LEADING THE
WAY TO
SUCCESS

Contents

Message from Publisher

There are many who want to lead and the reasons they want to lead are as varied as there are people who strive to be that person in front, showing the way. From genuinely wanting to help others to desiring status to making more money, there are many striving to get ahead by becoming a leader.

If you want to be a leader, the real question is, what is your real purpose for leading and in what direction do you intend to lead? We thought about this and other questions, and decided to gather several of the most successful leaders we could find to see how they lead and why.

The authors I interviewed gave me very insightful answers. One was: "The reality is that people *allow* us to lead and be influential when we're authentic and display transparency. I'm talking about being true to ourselves, and showing our true selves—telling the truth, walking our talk, and talking our walk with consistency."

Right away I knew I was on the right track and that this book was going to be a very helpful tool for our readers.

And then something else occurred to me—I do not have to be the president of a large corporation to be considered a leader. Everyone is a leader in some way. Being a leader is exercising influence on another. We all do it every day. Whether we lead others toward success by exhibiting good character traits or lead in another direction by exhibiting poor character traits, we are all leaders. The most rewarding experience, however, is to lead someone to success. The authors in this book will share their best tips and strategies on how to do just that.

I hope you enjoy reading this book as much as I enjoyed talking with these inspiring people. If you believe that failure is not an option, and if you have a genuine desire to continue your education about being the best leader you can be, this book will be a treasured addition to your library.

I extend to you my best wishes as you lead the way to success.

David Wright, President
International Speakers Network
& Insight Publishing

Chapter 1

Judy Nelson

THE INTERVIEW

David Wright (Wright)

Today, we're talking with Judy Nelson. Judy's philosophy about emotionally intelligent management derives from her unique educational background, a law degree, a master's degree in Social Work, training and certification as a professional coach, and thirty years as a coaching CEO. Now, as an executive coach and management trainer the payoff is exceptional. A coaching client who is a CEO commented, "If you're looking to make a change in your company or in your life, you should consider Judy Nelson's extensive experience, talents, and skills." Married to an amazing Menninger-trained psychiatrist, and a step-grandmother of eight, Judy is enjoying life to the fullest.

Judy, welcome to *Leading the Way to Success!*

Judy Nelson (Nelson)

Thank you David, I'm delighted to be here.

Wright

What is emotional intelligence?

Nelson

The simplest way for me to explain it is with a prayer from my Viking ancestors: "Dear Lord, keep your arm around my shoulder and one hand

1

over my mouth." The Vikings actually were praying for help with emotional intelligence!

Emotional intelligence (EQ) is the ability to act in ways that make us successful. In other words, emotional intelligence is the capacity to manage emotions and relationships. Peter Drucker believes that "a manager's job *is* relationships." Improving one's emotional intelligence is the best way to successfully create and maintain the positive relationships that are essential for a manager to be effective.

Wright

Why is emotional intelligence called EQ?

Nelson

It's also referred to as EI, which probably makes more sense. I think it's more commonly referred to as EQ because of the interconnection with intelligence quotient, or IQ. Emotional intelligence and IQ are very different, but they are both types of intelligences, and therefore, a relationship exists between the two.

Wright

How are EQ and IQ different?

Nelson

Your intelligence quotient is your capacity to learn—something you are born with. Generally speaking, your IQ is fixed. Emotional intelligence is a skill that can be improved with motivation, training, and a great deal of practice.

Wright

I learned that people who are really good at things are also very passionate about them. Why are you so passionate about EQ and emotional intelligence management?

Nelson

For one thing, EQ combines the management of emotions, thoughts, and behavior and that's really a big passion for me. I didn't always have a name for it, but all the conflict, gossip, mistrust, and disrespect that goes on in organizations, and particularly, in management teams, is often a product of a lack of awareness of how the three interrelate. That makes successful relationships a real problem. So for me, it's a framework for the intuitive practice that I've been using all along.

Wright

What is a more formal definition of emotional intelligence?

Nelson

There are several EQ experts, and their definitions of emotional intelligence differ a bit. I like to think of EQ as a person's ability to build and maintain positive relationships by knowing and handling emotions—your own and those around you.

Wright

Are there specific components or phases of emotional intelligence?

Nelson

There are four phases of EQ: self-awareness, self-management, social awareness, and relationship management. Very simple, but also, very complex.

Wright

Would you give our readers an example of someone who demonstrates a high EQ or EI?

Nelson

Basically, people with high emotional intelligence show grace under fire. They are in control of their impulses, and their behavior is intentional. Examples include Franklin Roosevelt, Gandhi, and more recently, GE's Jack Welch (in his role as CEO). On the celebrity end, Oprah comes across as being very much in charge of her emotions and skilled at building relationships.

In terms of the low end EQ, you can include people who are extremely impulsive, lose their temper, blame other people, and when in a management role are what might be described as *toxic* managers. Many of those CEOs who have gone to jail in recent years didn't display a very high

3

EQ. Jimmy Connors, the world champion tennis player, who acted out his anger every five minutes on the court, did not demonstrate a very high EQ.

A more recent example of low EQ was provided by the actor, Alec Baldwin, when his parental rage was made public in a loud cell phone conversation. National television replayed him yelling various epithets at his thirteen-year-old daughter, including calling her a "miserable little pig." Not exactly the stuff good father-daughter relationships are made of.

The antics of Britney Spears provide another extreme and very sad case of a well-known person who repeatedly demonstrates very low emotional intelligence in all four areas. (While there isn't space to discuss it here, it is important to note that sometimes emotional instability can cloud and/or complicate the emotional intelligence picture.)

Wright

Is there a secret to having a high EQ?

Nelson

I think there are three secrets actually, although the first one is a bit facetious. Number one is to choose your parents wisely! Children live what they learn, so if parents or caretakers model self-awareness and self-management as well as empathy and strong relationship skills, a child has a good chance of learning those techniques.

In my situation, I was taught two very negative lessons by my father, an immigrant and a judge by profession. The first was "do as I say, not as I do," which is really disastrous behavior for anybody in management. No manager can be effective unless words and behavior are in sync.

The other lesson my father attempted to instill in me was to never apologize. He saw it as a sign of weakness. This is another rather unhelpful lesson for an aspiring leader. It is vital that an executive model accountability for his or her behaviors, especially mistakes. An appropriate apology is a sign of strength, not weakness. Although he was a wise parent in other ways, I've had to unlearn those lessons over the years, and it hasn't been easy.

Wright

You said that there were three secrets to having a high EQ. What are the other two?

Nelson

The other two secrets are more practical. Secret number two is to have the willingness to "Fix You!" If you're not willing to work on yourself and what you can change, you're not going to be successful improving your EQ.

The third secret is practice. One of my favorite quotes says it all: "If you study math you become a mathematician; if you study history, you become a historian; and if you study swimming, you drown" *(author unknown)*. That's very true of emotional intelligence. You can't just read about it—you've got to practice, practice, practice.

Wright

I agree with what you said earlier—that it takes courage to work on improving one's emotional intelligence. Will you elaborate?

Nelson

Yes, I will. Many times I've encountered the crucial role that courage plays both in my professional and my personal life. Coming to terms with what you need to work on emotionally is really the ultimate in vulnerability—never a pleasant experience for any of us. But the courage to be vulnerable in this case can have a major payoff. You have to be willing to own your thoughts, your emotions, and your behavior. You have to be willing to admit mistakes and acknowledge the need for improvement, and you have to be willing to change and take risks. These are very difficult things for any of us to go through. As one author suggests, you have to "lean into the discomfort" in order to see any gain. That means tackling the toughest issues. However, if you persist, the end result can be transformational.

Wright

Is EQ the same as conflict management?

Nelson

Conflict management is a crucial aspect of emotional intelligence, but EQ is much broader. EQ focuses on building and maintaining positive relationships, and therefore, on preventing the conflict in the first place. It includes trustworthiness and whether you're conscientious or not. Conflict management, if you can master it, is certainly a major step toward increasing your emotional intelligence. Managing one's temper is an absolute basic skill required for any manager's success.

Wright

How would I determine whether a person has a high or a low EQ?

Nelson

There's no definitive test or magic number to signify a person's level of emotional intelligence. Unlike your IQ, EQ is not really an either/or concept; it's a continuum of your abilities and skills in different areas. When you see consistency, positive relationships, modeling values, that indicates a high EQ. Inconsistency, impulsivity, and demeaning behavior are all good indicators of a low EQ.

While emotional intelligence is not a fixed number, there are several useful assessments for EQ. The more reliable assessments (i.e. tests with large numbers of people) can capture where you stand on the four components at a certain point in time. Then you have specific areas that you can work on and benchmarks against which to compare your progress.

Finally, let me caution against ever using EQ-related concepts as a hammer. Labeling anyone is a dangerous strategy. The purpose of studying emotional intelligence is to find better ways to relate, not more varied ways to name-call.

Wright

So how is EQ different from emotional maturity?

Nelson

In many ways, it's not—in my book at least. There are several academics who distinguish emotional maturity as the next step after emotional intelligence. I really feel that emotional intelligence is so lacking that in my work with managers, I'll settle for a combination of the two. If we can increase the amount of EQ, we're going to be much closer to both emotional maturity and to making better managers and better human beings.

Not to complicate things, but the more I reflect on the role of emotional intelligence in organizations, the more I am convinced that to be willing to work on improving one's EQ requires a great deal of emotional maturity!

Wright

Isn't EQ pretty "touchy-feely" for the sophisticated executive?

Nelson

You bet. The reaction is often a glazed look, rolled eyes—or both! For a long time, I had a similar reaction. However, once I began to understand the amazing impact emotional intelligence has in the workplace, it wasn't possible to ignore—and that's usually true for even the most skeptical executive. A growing body of research shows solid evidence that a high EQ on the job is *directly* correlated to high performance—*and* to the bottom-line.

Wright

Tell us more about these studies.

Nelson

One organization studied half a million managers and identified the performance indicators that impact the bottom line. Emotional intelligence was one of the most significant factors in the study. It turns out that one's IQ or intellect is only *20 percent* of the factor in high performance; *emotional intelligence is 60 percent!* When executives hear the facts behind EQ, I find them to be much more receptive to it.

Before EQ can become widely accepted in the corporate world, we may have to come up with different language to describe it so that emotional intelligence doesn't sound so "soft." Still, right now, I am working with several executives, both in executive coaching and training, who are 100 percent onboard with the EQ concept because they have seen it work—for themselves and for their teams.

Wright

Will you elaborate on the basic elements of emotional intelligence?

Nelson

We talked about the four competencies a little earlier: self-awareness or insight, self-management, social awareness or empathy, and relationship management. I'd like to talk about each one separately, starting with self-awareness.

Wright

Is there a reason that self-awareness is first?

Nelson

Self-awareness, or insight, is not only the first competency, but also the first essential step in improving emotional intelligence. If you aren't aware of your feelings, attitudes, and emotional "triggers," you really can't be successful in reaching the ultimate goal of successfully managing relationships. Let me illustrate with an executive that I coached for over one year.

This senior manager always exceeded his annual goals. He received kudos about his high performance, but was not getting the raises he felt he deserved. He also received occasional complaints that he was more interested in results than in people but dismissed this feedback as misguided. Then, he learned the results of a company-mandated 360-degree assessment (multi-rater, anonymous review by peers, direct reports, etc.) for all managers.

This senior manager was shocked to learn that he was seen by most of his colleagues as intimidating and unpleasant to work with. That's when he asked for a coach. He had no clue that this was how he affected people. He came to me highly motivated to make whatever modifications were necessary to change the perception and to position him for career advancement.

Over several months as my executive coaching client, this executive made major strides in adjusting his self-perceptions and in paying more attention to the human side of the organization. He made such gigantic leaps that he's now getting extremely positive reviews in all areas, all because of increased self-awareness—and, of course, modified behavior. He was not previously aware that his behavior was a problem, even though there were several clues. Once he heard it formally from his colleagues, he changed his approach completely. He even started applying this new insight at home and reported positive changes in that environment as well.

Wright

Once a manager gets a handle on self-awareness, what's next?

Nelson

Self-management or self-regulation is the second aspect of emotional intelligence. Most people think of this as anger management focused on those individuals who need to control their tempers. That's important, but self-management is much more complicated. Let me give you an example.

Years ago I was sitting in the front row of a lecture hall listening very intently to a nationally known speaker. I was struggling to understand what he was saying because it was complex. All of a sudden he stopped and said to me, "Why are you so angry?"

Startled, I said, "I'm not angry, I'm just concentrating."

He said, "Well, concentrate without frowning. You're distracting me completely. Now where was I?" And he picked up his speech notes and continued.

The speaker's lack of impulse control and self-management was pretty obvious and a good indication of how his lack of EQ caused him to shoot himself in the foot. The audience was so annoyed at the way he treated me that nobody bought his books after the lecture!

The real issue for me was about my own lack of emotional intelligence. Before that evening, I had no idea that I was a frowner or that it could be distracting to other people. Once I knew, I became very conscious of my tendency to wrinkle my brow when concentrating. That awareness has helped me to be more in control of my facial expressions and other body language—and a more successful leader as a result. (However, it would have been a lot less painful if that speaker had exercised more emotional intelligence and pulled me aside after the speech instead of in the middle of it!)

Wright

That covers knowing and managing ourselves. What about those around us?

Nelson

Awareness of how others are feeling (i.e., social awareness) is the third element. I prefer the term "empathy" because it seems more comprehensive. Empathy is often defined as "standing in another's shoes." While that's one way to think about it, again, empathy is more than that. It's trying to understand another person's challenges, feelings, and what the problem might look like from his or her point of view.

When you think this way, you are going to be more successful in relating to that person, if for no other reason than because it's not all about you. The critical issue here is never to assume that we fully understand another person. Therefore, it is usually helpful to check our assumptions by asking questions.

I would like to give you a personal example of empathy, or rather lack of it, in action. When I was in graduate school many years ago, I hadn't gained the benefit of emotional maturity or emotional intelligence. I really thought I knew everything there was to know. You couldn't tell me anything.

I was a first-year social work intern in a large inner-city public health department. On my second day in the office, I loudly berated a secretary because she hadn't done something that I thought she should have done. My supervisor (also the dean's wife) overheard the exchange, called me into her office, and told me to take a seat.

After a long pause she asked, "Are you planning to graduate?"

"Of course I am!" I said, indignantly. She informed me that if she ever heard me talk to anybody like that again, she would see that I didn't graduate from that or any other school. It was pretty harsh feedback, but I definitely learned that nobody is insignificant in an organizational setting and that having empathy for other people was a bottom line for building relationships, personal and professional alike.

Wright

You've said that the fourth element of emotional intelligence is also the ultimate goal for managers. Will you explain?

Relationship management is indeed the ultimate goal because relationships are the key to success on the job—and in life. Another way to think about it is as "strategic social skills." In other words, to be successful you need to manage yourself in order to foster essential relationships.

Earlier I mentioned the example of Alec Baldwin's extremely rude and verbally abusive behavior toward his daughter. That behavior certainly didn't award Mr. Baldwin many points in any aspect of the emotional intelligence arena, but I think he scored the lowest in both self-control and relationship management. I wish him luck in trying to rebuild his relationship with his daughter, the most important relationship a parent can have.

Unfortunately, there are too many managers out there who behave like Alec Baldwin (although I'm sure that doesn't include our readers!). Wouldn't it be nice if those kinds of managers understood that the real bottom line is to be sure that their perceptions of themselves are accurate, that they must manage their emotions, empathize with others, and strategically relate to those they work with if there is to be any hope of building positive and long-term relationships? If those elements can be mastered, it's called personal effectiveness—the ultimate management success!

Wright

Aren't most successful managers self-aware?

Nelson

To tell you the truth, many of them think they are, but they're not. If they are highly successful, they may not think there is any need for self-awareness or they think they are already very self-aware.

However, our perceptions of ourselves are obviously one-sided. *The only way to get accurate information about how others perceive you is to ask.*

Another key issue is that people are often afraid to give "the boss" feedback. The result can be that the executive believes his or her own press and may be totally ignorant of how he or she is impacting others. Only through anonymous multi-rater feedback can the boss be sure of receiving honest input.

Wright

The second phase of EQ is self-management. Is that not the same as self-control?

Nelson

Self-control is a major part of self-management, but as we discussed earlier, there are many more components. One critical element is trustworthiness or values. Do you practice what you preach? Are you adaptable and flexible? When handling change, are you conscientious? Do you take responsibility for your own actions? Are you open to new ideas? Self-control is an important part of self-management, but far from the total picture.

Wright

Can you give our readers greater insight into empathy? That's not an easy task.

Nelson

Without empathy, we can't have positive, lasting relationships. Empathy is the absolute key to being able to sense another's feelings, and to trying to understand another's perspective. It means moving outside of ourselves to think about the other person.

Other areas of empathy include a "service orientation," where you're anticipating the needs of others and offering assistance; and mentoring, where you're helping others develop and build their own skills. Empathy also includes the ability to relate well to people of different cultures and ethnicities. Finally, there is a need for attunement to the group's needs and points of view.

Empathy is critical to successful relationships but effectiveness still assumes self-awareness and self-management first.

Wright

The final phase, relationship management, standing on its own, almost sounds to me like manipulation.

Nelson

That's a really good point because in some cases, it can be. In the case of the demagogues like Hitler and Mussolini, they trampled on all four of the EQ elements to take advantage of others and to do unspeakably savage things. Relationship management can be manipulation, but the whole idea of emotional intelligence is to develop positive and long-lasting relationships so that manipulation would not have a role. EQ is a way to manage the conversation and interaction in order to foster relationships. The bottom line is what kind of relationship do you want with that other person, and how do you go about making that happen?

Wright

Given the four phases, which do you think is the most important?

Nelson

They're all critical for success, but again, self awareness and personal insight top the list. I like the quote: "Our greatest adversary is our own ignorance." Without self-awareness, people are literally loose cannons, shooting their mouths off whenever they're the least bit annoyed or frustrated and totally unaware of how their thoughts and feelings drive their behavior and how that impacts others, usually in a negative way.

There are people who are successful without emotional intelligence, but they've missed opportunities. Those who are successful without emotional intelligence have not realized their full potential. They have no idea how much more successful they could be.

Wright

Which phase of emotional intelligence is the hardest for most people to improve?

Nelson

At the risk of being repetitive, I have to go back to self-awareness. Self-management isn't easy, but self-awareness means changing how you view yourself. It means taking responsibility, not blaming anybody else—not your parents, not your boss, not your spouse. The ultimate pain is in owning your own stuff, admitting it, and being willing to fix it. In my management trainings, I call it "Fix You First!"

Wright

I must admit, insight and introspection are not my two greatest qualities. They're hard!

Nelson

That's true for so many people, but once you take the plunge, *in a safe place*, it's amazing how much more conscious control you can have over your life and how much more successful you will be. That's why more and more executives are seeking coaching. They want a partner they trust to help them discover positive strategies to make essential but difficult personal changes.

Before we move on, I'd like to elaborate on how important it is for conversations about emotional intelligence growth to take place in a safe environment. Someone once said "Stress makes people stupid!" I couldn't agree more. If feedback about one's performance is perceived as criticism or an attack, the individual will not be able to hear anything else, much less engage in a rational conversation. Managers must find ways to give non-demeaning feedback that focuses on improvable behaviors, not on the person's worth or lack thereof.

Wright

Are there some people who refuse to work on improving their EQ?

Nelson

Oh yes. In their minds, they believe they are right, everybody else is wrong, and others are to blame for their negative situations. Some have ignored blatant cues along the way. For others, no one has had the courage/skill to give them feedback, so they assume that they're right.

Years ago, I hired a fundraising director who came highly recommended for his skills in raising money. On the second day on the job, he was talking to me in the hallway when he spotted a major donor at the other end of the hall. He cut me off in midsentence and almost knocked over three people as he raced to get to her.

When I called him on it, he reminded me how much money she had and that I didn't understand. I warned him that his behavior violated the basic values of the organization and could not be repeated. The next day, he did something similar. I called him into my office and repeated the earlier warning. Then I offered to work with him to modify his behavior, but he told me that he didn't need to change. Needless to say, that was his last day as an employee.

To improve one's EQ, one has to be motivated. You cannot force someone to work on his or her emotional intelligence.

Wright

Am I not getting it or do you seem to be suggesting that we hire based on a person's EQ?

Nelson

I do believe a person's EQ is one of several factors to be considered in a hiring situation, but never the only one. Certainly the individual has to have the basic intellect and innate talent to do the job. Experience is usually a critical factor as well. But if you hire an individual who is rude to direct reports, arrogant with peers, and generally mistreats people, it doesn't matter what skills he or she has or how wonderful his or her references are. Unless the job description does not include working with people, this is not the right person to hire.

To help me find the right person for a management position, I have developed an interesting tool to use in hiring situations that allows me to informally test for qualities of emotional intelligence. It's based on my agreement with the author of a Harvard Business School article who said that the sign of a good manager is the ability to give and receive negative feedback. I also think it's a good indicator of emotional intelligence.

In interviews with applicants for management level jobs, and sometimes other levels, I ask the candidates to role-play situations with me where they have to give difficult feedback to a direct report, which is the role I play. Then I reverse it and role-play where they have to receive difficult feedback from me, playing a supervisor. If feasible, I videotape (with consent, of course) the role-playing and replay it for us to watch together. The way they respond provides valuable fodder for further conversation. This technique highlights all four areas of EQ and is very useful.

Wright

So if managers are highly skilled in all of the EQ areas, then what?

Nelson

Well, the odds of professional and personal success soar. Relationships are positive, and they are modeling positive behaviors. Individuals with high EQ acknowledge that they still have room for improvement—another good example for staff.

Our readers may recall Abraham Maslow's Hierarchy of Needs where he identified five key stages to personal and self-development: physiological, safety, social, self-esteem and self-actualization. I think individuals who are strongly skilled in EQ are approaching a state of being self-actualized, the highest stage in Maslow's Hierarchy of Needs.

Individuals who are fully self-actualized (and the numbers are relatively small) feel in control of their lives and find an ultimate happiness in that control. Why? Because they are doing what they want to do in a positive way. In other words, they have achieved *inner peace*. I think that's what most of us are yearning for.

Wright

So why is learning EQ skills so difficult for so many?

Nelson

Some people grow up with powerful beliefs that they absorbed from their parents or learned in school, and these are extremely difficult to give up or to change. Others have a big ego or pride that is interfering with an acknowledgement of their role in their own destiny. Some are mature in years but not in emotions.

While it's true that most of us become more emotionally intelligent as we age, that is not always the case.

Teenagers and young adults are often grappling with their own issues and are unable to really focus on these areas. In addition, if they have a tendency to get defensive, they can't hear what anybody else has to say. They can't take in that feedback because their mind is too busy defending why what they're doing is the right way. And if you can't accept feedback, you can't learn or grow.

Wright

As you were talking, I was lamenting the fact that I think my EQ has probably gotten stronger throughout the years, but that I wish I had known about this years ago so it wouldn't have taken age and wisdom to work it out.

Nelson

Isn't that the truth for all of us? The whole point is that with a higher level of emotional intelligence we can perform better with less angst and much more fun. It's a shame that some of us have waited so long, but it's never too late! That's one of the many reasons I so enjoy coaching and training bright and motivated managers and management teams. Frankly, my hope is that I can help them figure this stuff out a lot sooner and with far less pain than you and I had to endure!

Wright

How will higher EQ skills affect managers and management teams?

Nelson

The fact is that it's just more fun to go to work when people have higher emotional intelligence as managers and management teams. There is less tension and greater respect; there's more time for real work. People are focused on teamwork, the bottom line, and the mission, instead of hassling with interpersonal issues all day.

Word spreads about agencies with this kind of a culture and more talented people seek out these organizations. And talk about retention! People *want* to stay in organizations that value them, that help with their personal growth, and where there isn't a lot of fighting going on all of the time. Who needs that?

Wright

Sounds like you think everyone needs to improve their EQ, even children?

Nelson

That's exactly what I believe, starting with me! We commented on it earlier—why do we have to wait so long to figure this stuff out? What if in school during interpersonal conflicts, you and I had been asked to reflect on our feelings and how we were affecting other people? And what if we had gotten coaching in a safe way—a safe place—to focus on how we could improve? What if on the job we had received constructive and respectful feedback on the spot instead of with the annual performance review nine months later? I think the world would be a very different place.

As a footnote, I believe that most annual performance reviews are more detrimental than motivating; I would like to see the whole system of performance review reinvented. Too often employees receive little or no feedback during the year. Then, in the annual review, they are admonished for something they did wrong nine months ago and now they can't even remember the situation.

Wright

So is there anything else we haven't covered?

Nelson

Actually, we've only skimmed the surface of emotional intelligence, so I would encourage our readers to explore the topic further. The Web site is loaded with good resources, and I would be glad to respond to inquiries.

To recap, the central rationale for a manger to improve his or her emotional intelligence comes from Peter Drucker: "A manager's job is relationships—upwards, downwards, sideways." Improving one's emotional intelligence is the most effective way I have found to make those relationships work.

The most important concept that I would like our readers to remember is that emotional intelligence is a learned ability, and therefore, we can keep learning and improving it for a lifetime.

To be successful, we need to constantly think about all four aspects of emotional intelligence as we are going through our daily lives. And, in order to live and work to our full capacity, we need to practice identifying, using, understanding, and managing our emotions—over and over and over again. As one of my coaching clients recently said when her husband responded positively to her changed behavior, "This stuff really works!"

I'd like to conclude by revisiting that prayer from my Viking ancestors, essentially asking their Maker to restrain their impulses. What if they'd learned to put their own arm around their shoulders and their own hands over their mouths? Their behavior would certainly have been more civilized. Their example might even have led to better press for Vikings, more emotional intelligence in the world, and thus better relationships.

My conviction is that if we all improved our emotional intelligence it would positively impact our success as managers, spouses, and as human beings. It would also contribute to the bottom line and hopefully, even the world's peace.

Wright

What a great conversation. I really enjoyed our talk. I've learned a lot, and I've got a lot to think about here.

Today we've been talking with Judy Nelson. Her philosophy about emotionally intelligent management stems from her unique background in her education and her experience. Now I know why a law degree, a master's degree in Social Work, training and certification as a professional coach, and her thirty years of work as a coaching CEO has led her to some of these great things that she's been talking about. I hope you readers have taken in as much as I have today.

Judy, thank you so much for being with us today on *Leading the Way to Success!*

Nelson

Thank you, David; it was truly a privilege.

About the Author

Judy Nelson's philosophy about emotionally intelligent management derives from her unique educational background, a law degree, a master's degree in Social Work, training and certification as a professional coach, and thirty years as a coaching CEO. Now, as an executive coach and management trainer the payoff is exceptional. A coaching client who is a CEO commented, "If you're looking to make a change in your company or in your life, you should consider Judy Nelson's extensive experience, talents, and skills."

Married to an amazing Menninger-trained psychiatrist, and a step-grandmother of eight; Judy is enjoying life to the fullest.

Judy Nelson
361 Calle Mayor
Redondo Beach, California 90277
877.yesJudy
Judy@coachjudynelson.com
www.coachjudynelson.com

Chapter 2

Dr. Warren Bennis

THE INTERVIEW

David E. Wright (Wright)

Today we are talking with Dr. Warren Bennis, Ph.D. He is a university professor and a distinguished professor of business at the University of Southern California and chairman of USC's leadership institute. He has written eighteen books, including *On Becoming A Leader*, *Why Leaders Can't Lead*, and *The Unreality Industry*, coauthored with Ivan Mentoff. Dr. Bennis was successor to Douglas McGregor as chairman of the organizational studies department at MIT. He also taught at Harvard and Boston universities. Later he was provost and executive vice president of the State University of New York—Buffalo and president of the University of Cincinnati. He published over 900 articles and two of his books have earned the coveted McKenzie Award for the "Best Book on Management." He has served in an advisory capacity for the past four U.S. presidents, and consultant to many corporations and agencies and to the United Nations. Awarded eleven honorary degrees, Dr. Bennis has also received numerous awards including the Distinguished Service Award from the American Board of Professional Psychologists and the Perry L. Ruther Practice Award from the American Psychological Association.

Dr. Bennis, welcome to *Leading the Way to Success*.

Bennis

I'm glad to be here again with you, David.

Wright

In a conversation with *Behavior Online*, you stated that most organizations devaluate potential or emerging leaders by seven criteria: business literacy, people skills, conceptual abilities, track record, taste, judgment, and character. Because these terms were somewhat vague, you left them to be defined by the reader. Can we give our readers an unadorned definition of these criteria, as you define them?

Bennis

There's no precise dictionary definition that would satisfy me or maybe anyone. I'll just review them very quickly because there's a lot more we want to discuss.

Business literacy really means: do you know the territory, do you know the ecology of the business, do you know how it works, do you know where the plugs are, do you know who the main stakeholders are, and are you familiar with a thing called business culture.

People skills: This is your capacity to connect and engage, because business leadership is about establishing, managing, creating, and engaging in relationships. Conceptual abilities is more important these days because it has to do with the paradoxes and complexities—the cartography—of stakeholders that make life at the top (more than ever) interesting and difficult, which is why we've had such a turnover in CEOs and leaders over the last few years.

Track record: Now, if I want to know about a person—if I were a therapist—one of the first questions I would ask is, "Tell me about your job history." That tells me a lot. On the whole, as my Dad used to say, "People who get A's are smart." People who have a successful track record tend to be effective. We don't always go on that, because sometimes these people don't grow. But, if I had only one measuring stick, it would be that one: Tell me your job history. Let's talk about whether it looks successful or whether you view it as successful or not. It's hard to define, but it's about whether or not you have the capacity a good curator has, a good selector has, to know people. It's always a tough one; God knows we all make mistakes. Your taste means your capacity to judge other people in relation to the other six characteristics.

I think taste and judgment are combined. I dealt with them separately because I thought taste was specifically the selection of people in an intuitive and objective way, but also in a subjective way. It has to do with the range of such things as being bold versus being reckless. It has to do with the strategic implications and consequences of any decision and what you take into account in making any decision, especially the tough ones. The easy ones are different; everyone looks good in a bull market. It's when things get tough, vulnerable, difficult, and in a crisis mode that judgment really counts the most. Taste and judgment are the hardest things to learn, let alone teach.

Character: Here I have in mind a variety of things such as size of ego, the capacity to listen, emotional intelligence, integrity, and authenticity. Basically, is this a person I can trust? That's what character is all about.

Wright

You said that businesses get rid of their top leaders because of lapses in judgment, and lapses in character, not because of business literacy or conceptual skills. Why do you think this is true?

Bennis

It's true simply because it's true. Look at the record. I wasn't just stating a hypothesis there that looks to be proved. I was stating experiences with leaders and I'll give you three quick examples.

Let's take a recent one. Howell Raines had the top job in journalism in the world. He had great ideas, great business literacy, and all the things in the top five. He did not have taste, judgment, or character. This is a guy who had an ego the size of Texas. He played favorites, had the best ideas, was a terrific newspaperman and no one would argue with that. But, his way of treating people—of not harnessing the human harvest that was there, and his bullying, brutalizing, arrogant behavior and his inability to to listen; that's what I mean by character.

Eckhart Pfeiffer was fired after seven or eight very good years at Compaq. He had terrific ideas, but he did not listen to the people. He was only listening to those on his "A" list who were saying, "Aye, aye, sir."

People on his "B" list were saying, "You'd better look at what Gateway and Dell are doing; they're eating our lunch on our best china." He didn't listen; he didn't want to listen. That's what I mean by character. Let me just stay with those two examples, I don't think it's ever about conceptual abilities—ever. There may be some examples I just don't know about. But, with over fifty years of leadership research, I don't know of any leader who has lost his job or has been ousted because of a lack of brainpower.

Wright

You said that teaching leadership is impossible, but you also said leadership can be learned. How can that be?

Bennis

Let me qualify that. I teach the stuff, so no, it isn't impossible to teach you. As is the case with everything, teaching and learning are two different things. One has to do with input into people; the other has to do with whether or not they get it. You know very well, and your listeners and readers know very well, that there's a difference between listening to a lecture and it having any influence on you. You can listen to a brilliant lecture and nothing may happen. So, there's a disconnect to teaching and learning.

Actually, how people learn about leadership varies a lot. Most people don't learn about leadership by getting a Ph.D., or by reading a book, or by listening to a tape, although that may be helpful. They learn it through work and experience. You can be helped by terrific teaching from a recording, a tape, a book, or a weekend retreat.

Basically, the way people learn about leadership is by keeping their eyes open, being a first-class noticer, having good role models and being able to see how they deal with life's adversities. You don't learn leadership by reading books. They are helpful, don't get me wrong. I write books; I want them to be read. The message you are trying to get out to your people, to listen to and to read is also important. I think it's terrific. That's my life's work. That's what I do for a living, and I love it. I'll tell you, it has to be augmented by the experiences you face in work and in life.

Wright

Trust me, I have learned, after reading many of your books, that they are teaching materials.

Bennis

Thank-you. I hope you also learn from them, David.

Wright

As I was reading those books, I wondered why I did the things you said to do, and they worked when I did it. It's simply because I learned by doing.

Bennis

Thank-you. I'm really glad to hear that.

Wright

Since leadership is where the big money, prestige, and power is, why would seasoned business executives, who are monitored more closely than the average employee, let character issues bring them down? One would think it would be like a person who constantly uses profanity, just deciding not to curse in church.

Bennis

I wish it were that easy. It's a really good question. I wish I knew the answer, but I don't. I will give you a real quick example. Howell Raines, as I said before, executive editor of the *New York Times* (people would die to get that position) was an experienced newspaperman, and there was a 17,000-word article about him in *New Yorker*, June 6, 2002 (he had been on the job since September 2001, so it was written not a year later). The article exposed him; it was a very frank and interesting article. It called him arrogant, a bully, playing favorites, all the things I said earlier, and also called him a hell of a good man and a terrific editor. He'd been around the track; he had business literacy up the wah-zoo. He was as good as they get.

He read that article and everybody at the *New York Times* read it. Do you think it might have made him want to change a little bit? Did Julius Caesar not hear the warnings, "Beware the Ides of March?" Did he not hear, "Don't go to the forum?" There were so many signals and he wasn't listening. Why wasn't he listening? Didn't he go down to the newsroom and

25

talk to those people? No. The most common and fatal error is that because of arrogance; they stopped listening. It could happen internally, as in the case of Howell Raines, or like Eckhart Pfeiffer, who wasn't listening to his "B" list tell him about Gateway and Dell.

I don't have the answer to your question, but I will tell you, someone ought to be around to remind these people of the voices, stakeholders, and audiences they aren't listening to. That's a way of dealing with it—making sure you have a trusted staff that isn't just giving you the good news.

Wright

I've often heard that if I had been Nixon, I would have burned the tapes, apologized, and moved on.

Bennis

Absolutely.

Wright

I think it's the arrogance factor; you really "hit the nail on the head" when you said that, to put it in my simple terms.

How does one experience leadership when they haven't yet become a leader?

Bennis

How do you become a parent for the first time? There's no book that you are going to read on becoming a parent any more than there is a book you are going to read on becoming a leader that will prepare you for that experience. You're going to fall on your face, get up, dust yourself off, and go on. The only thing you're going to learn from is your experiences and having someone around you can depend on for straight, reflective back-talk. A lot of it is breaks, and chance. Some of it isn't that, but if there's one thing I want to underscore, nobody is prepared the first time they are going to be in the leadership position. You're going to fall on your face, you're going to learn from it, and you're going to continue that for the rest of your life.

Wright

At one time, I had a company with about 175 people working for me; we had business in the millions. I just kept making so many mistakes that afterward, I did wish I had read some of the things you had written about before I made those mistakes. It sure would have been helpful.

In your studies, you found that failure, not success, had a greater impact on future leaders—leaders learn the most by facing adversity. Do you think teachers at the college level make this clear?

Bennis

I can't speak for all teachers at the college level. Do you mean people teaching leadership and business management at the college level?

Wright

Yes.

Bennis

I don't know if they do. But, I would imagine things are much more difficult and complicated today because of the kinds of things that business leaders are facing such as: globalization, fierce Darwinian competitiveness, complexity of the problems, regulatory pressures, changes in demography, difficulty of retaining your best talent, the price of terrific human capital and then keeping them, the ability to help create a climate that encourages collaboration, and then there's the world danger since 9/11.

Wright

In my case, I just remember the equations and things in the courses I took, such as controlling and directing and those kinds of things. I don't remember anybody ever telling me about exit strategies or what's going to happen if my secretary gets pregnant and my greatest salesperson is the one responsible for it. Who do I fire? As the owner of a small company that's growing at a rapid pace, what can I do to facilitate the competencies of the people I have chosen to lead this into the future?

Bennis

Your company is how big, again?

Wright

I was talking before about a real estate conglomerate. Presently I have a speakers' bureau/servicing agency and publishing business. I employ about twenty-five people, and we also use about fifty vendors, which I look at as employees.

Bennis

Yes, they are, aren't they? That's a good way of thinking about it. There are several things you can do in any size company, but with a small company, you can get your arms around it—conceptually, anyway. The leader/owner has to model the very behaviors he wants others to model. If you are espousing something that is antithetical to your behavior, then that's going to be a double bind. That's number one.

The second thing is to make leadership development an organic part of the activities at the firm. In addition to encouraging people to read, bringing in people to talk to them, and having retreats, every once in a while, look at leadership competencies and what people can do to sharpen and enhance those capacities that are needed to create a culture where people can openly talk about these issues. All of those things can be used to create a climate where leadership development is a part of the everyday dialogue.

Wright

If you were helping me choose people to assume leadership roles as my company grows, what characteristics would you suggest I look for?

Bennis

I've implied some of them early on as we discussed those seven characteristics. I've become a little leery of the whole selection process; there is some evidence that even interviews don't give you really valid insight. I think what I would tend to do is look at the track record. Talk about that with the person, where they think they have failed, where they think they have succeeded. Try to get a sense of their capacity to reflect on issues and see to what extent they have been able to learn from their previous experiences.

See what you can make of how realistically they assess a situation. Most people rarely attribute any blame to themselves; they always think, "The dog ate my homework." It's always some other agent outside of themselves who is to blame. Those are the things that I think are going to be characteristics of emerging leaders among men and women. That's what I would look for—the capacity to reflect and learn.

Wright

When you made that comment about interviews, I don't feel as inept as I did before this conversation. I'm sixty-four years old and the longer I live, I just feel that when people come in and interview, I want to give them an Academy Award as they walk out. People can say almost anything convincingly in this culture. It's very, very difficult for me to get through, so that's one thing I really had not thought of. It seems so simple though—just follow the track record.

Bennis

I have had the same experience you've had. When I was president of the university and making lots of choices all the time, my best was hitting 700, which means I was off three out of ten times. I think my average here was 60/40; it's rough. It's even harder these days because of legal restrictions, how much you can say about their references, how much they can reveal. We have to pay attention to selection level, no kidding. We can overcome mistakes in the selection level by the culture and how it will screen out behaviors that are not acceptable. That's our best default—the culture itself will so educate people that even mistakes we make will be resurrected by the culture being our best friend and ally.

Wright

As a leader, generating trust is essential. You have written extensively on this subject. Can you give our readers some factors that tend to generate trust?

Bennis

People want a leader who exudes that they know what he/she is doing. They want a doctor who is competent and they want a boss who really knows their way around. Secondly, you want someone who is really on your side—a caring leader. Thirdly, you want a leader who has directness, integrity, congruity, who returns calls, and is trustworthy, who will be there when needed and cares about you and about your growth. Those are the main things. It's not just individuals involved.

A boss must create a climate within the group that provides psychological safety—a holding pattern where people feel comfortable in speaking openly. I think that's another key factor in generating and establishing trust.

Wright

It is said that young people these days have less hope than their parents. What can leaders do to instill hope in their employees?

Bennis

All (and you can emphasize *all*) the leaders I have known have a high degree of optimism and a low degree of pessimism. They are, as Confucius said, "purveyors of hope." Look at Reagan, in a way look at Clinton, and Martin Luther King, Jr. These are people who have held out an idea of what we could become and made us proud of ourselves, created noble aspirations, sometimes audacious, but noble. Leaders have to express in an authentic way that there is a future for our nation and that you have a part in developing that future with me.

Wright

Dr. Bennis, thank you for being with us today, and for taking so much time to answer these questions.

Bennis

Thank you for having me.

About the Author

Warren Bennis has written or edited twenty-seven books, including the best-selling *Leaders* and *On Becoming A Leader*; both of which have been translated into twenty-one languages. He has served on four U.S. presidential advisory boards and has consulted for many Fortune 500 companies, including General Electric, Ford, and Starbucks. The *Wall Street Journal* named him one of the top ten speakers on management in 1993 and 1996, and *Forbes* magazine referred to him as "the dean of leadership gurus."

Warren Bennis
m.christian@marshall.usc.edu

Dr. Warren Bennis

Chapter 3

Dr. Kevin F. Hub

THE INTERVIEW

David Wright (Wright)

Today we're talking with Dr. Kevin F. Hub. Kevin brings more than twenty years of leadership and management experience to his clients. His personal vision is to have the greatest impact possible on the growth and development of others. He specializes in the personal development of current and aspiring leaders and is the creator of the "Assistance for Assistants" leadership development program. With an expertise in leadership education, his active, engaging style produces results that have an immediate impact on the leadership development of his audience. Dr. Hub is a graduate of the United States Military Academy and served with distinction on the front lines in Desert Storm. He lives in Richmond, Kentucky, with his wife and three children.

Dr Hub, welcome to *Leading the Way to Success*.

Kevin F. Hub (Hub)

Thank you, David.

Wright

You're a graduate of the United States Military Academy at West Point, arguably one of the most prestigious institutions of leadership in the world. How have your experiences at West Point shaped your development as a leader?

Hub

I am asked that question often and one of the first responses I give is that not a single day passes when I don't reflect on my experiences at West Point. I think specifically, David, that the volume and variety of leadership experiences that I have been exposed to and the times when I've had to make decisions that affect dozens (and sometimes hundreds) of other people, as well as the expectation to learn while leading, have given me a unique perspective.

When I talk about the volume and variety of leadership experiences I faced, I'm referring to my time as a cadet, where it was imperative to balance academics, athletics, and military responsibilities, as well as my time as an infantry officer in the United States Army serving in both peace time and war time.

In the years since my honorable discharge from the Army, every single day is made easier because I am able to use the leadership intuition I have developed over the last twenty years. I think that unique perspective allows me to make decisions, to lead by example, and to set expectations that might not otherwise be so easy for me without the experiences I've had at West Point and in the Army.

Wright

You seem so passionate about leadership and leadership development. Would you describe for our readers the value you place on developing others?

Hub

You know, David, there has been an ages-old discussion regarding whether leadership is an art or a science. I am going to say that I think clearly leadership is both, but the greatest portion is science. I value and am very passionate about the importance of continual development as a leader. I think the toughest, but most important thing for leaders to do is to develop others. John Maxwell says that "a leader's lasting value is measured by succession." I think it's crucial for leaders to make sure that they are always developing others.

Management theory asks, "When is it worth five hours to save five minutes?" As leaders, it is worth every minute to develop those you lead so that they can successfully lead when you leave. We have many examples in the corporate world—too numerous to mention—where succession plans have worked and companies have moved on and not skipped a beat. There are other instances where succession plans were not even in place and we've seen entire turnovers and even bankruptcies occur because leaders did not have that passion for developing others.

Wright

What do you see as the secret to leadership success in the twenty-first century?

Hub

Here's what I'd like for our readers to think about as they read this chapter:

- Do you think that effective leaders for the twenty first century need to fix their weaknesses?
- Do you think that successful leaders in the twenty-first century need to build teams of well-rounded individuals?
- Do you think that successful leaders in the twenty-first century need to set high expectations?
- Do they need to motivate others?
- Should they build consensus and delegate tasks?

If the readers of this book are like many of the crowds I've spoken to in the past, the majority answer "yes" to every one of those questions. But, David, I'm going to say just the opposite. I think that leadership success in the twenty-first century is not about fixing weaknesses—it's about building strengths. It's not about building teams of well-rounded individuals; but rather, it's about building teams of individuals with specific talents. It's not about setting high expectations for those they lead, it's about setting the right expectations. It's not about motivating others, it's about inspiring others. It's not about building consensus, it's about making informed decisions. Lastly, it's not about delegating tasks, it's about empowering others.

As our readers reflect on what I've just said, let me share a six-step process that leads the way to success. I think it's important for leaders to create a leadership profile. I think it's important for them to build a team. I think it's important for them to set expectations and then lead by example. I think it's important to make decisions and lastly, to monitor progress on decisions that have been made.

Wright

With so many people confident that fixing weaknesses is a sure-fire way to increase performance, why do you think the strengths perspective is the only way to go?

Hub

I think it's impossible to lead others when you can't lead yourself. I think too often leaders imitate the qualities of a mentor rather than developing their own leadership principles and leadership characteristics. Additionally, I think leaders focus on the growth and development of others before carefully creating their own leadership profile. Without self-control, emotional self-awareness, and accurate self-assessment, leaders have difficulty creating their own personal leadership profile.

Part of that self-assessment is accurately identifying talents. We need to identify talents that can be turned into strengths with experience and education, instead of trying to fix our weaknesses. I think the strengths perspective is the only way to go. It's as simple as human nature. Don't we like to do things that we do well better than doing things that we don't do well?

It's seen with athletes and it's seen with hobbyists who focus on the things they do well instead of fixing their weaknesses. That is a huge paradigm shift in my organization. In organizations I consult with, the professional development plans of leaders, managers, directors, coordinators—people in all positions—are designed to help employees fix their weaknesses.

Let's use a scale of one to ten. No one can afford to have somebody who's at a four in a certain skill or characteristic spend months improving that skill to be a seven. We cannot afford to have sevens in our organization. You cannot afford to have sevens in your organization. Let's focus on where they are at the level of seven, and make them all level tens. I think all of us would agree that we want organizations filled with tens.

Wright

Assessing talent is a critical attribute for the very best leaders. How do the very best leaders develop their teams?

Hub

As I mentioned, I think a lot of people have come to believe that building teams of well-rounded individuals is the way to go. And I'm going to disagree. I think I want a well-rounded team with individuals who have honed their skills to razor sharpness. And they can do that by focusing on their strengths. And again, that goes back to having a very acute sense of self-awareness and accurate self-assessment.

David, I think after creating their leadership profile, successful leaders must build a team. As leaders, we're naturally more comfortable in the company of people like ourselves, but we must avoid that. It's only human nature to surround ourselves with people who have the same leadership aptitudes and leadership characteristics that we have. It's also human nature to flock toward leaders who have those same aptitudes and characteristics, but productive tension results when team members see issues differently and when they approach issues differently. It's important to consider skills that you already have, but then train people to complement those skills.

I think successful leaders in the twenty-first century must build well-rounded teams with individuals who have very specific talents.

Wright

Many of us have been led to believe that high expectations yield high results. Yet you have said you don't think leaders should set high expectations. Would you explain that for our readers?

Hub

I can usually predict the success of a workshop or a guest speaking opportunity if I am able to keep people in the room after I tell them that I do not embrace the concept of leaders setting high expectations. If I can keep them in their seats after making that comment, then I know I have them hooked.

I think JoAnn Miller, from the Gallup Organization, says it best: "High expectations are a hope, but the right expectations are a plan."

I'll relate it to the classroom teacher. I don't think classroom teachers do their students justice when they walk in the very first day and say, "We are all going to be successful, and we are all going to learn to read by Christmas." Well, there are students in that classroom who will learn faster. Learning to read by Christmas is going to have them moving at a snail's pace because by Labor Day they are ready to read. Other students in the classroom will be more challenged by the deadline. Having them read by Christmas is going to produce such stress that it may show up in illness or a medical condition because they're just not able to meet the deadline.

Here is the concept in a sports analogy. My son was a very successful wrestler as a freshman in a very large high school in Kentucky. I didn't think it was the right expectation for his coach to tell him, "You are such a good wrestler you can make it to the state tournament." As a ninth-grader wrestling varsity, he was not going to make it to the state tournament. And when he didn't make it to the state tournament, it was difficult to see him break down and to see all the disappointment he felt because he thought he failed. Maybe the right expectation would have been, "win every match against other freshmen and win half of your matches against the upper classmen."

What's important is the distinction between "right" expectations, that are very specific and very keenly identified with the individual, and generic "high" expectations that are blindly cast across an organization without regard to individual differences. I am not advocating a lower standard; instead, I'm suggesting that successful leaders in the twenty-first century inspire others to set the right expectations based on their unique talents and skills.

Wright

Many leaders attribute their success to motivating others and being a "people person." Why do you take such exception to this way of thinking?

Hub

David, I'd ask the readers to consider if there is ever a situation when being a "people person" is not an attribute of an effective leader. I can think of none. Therefore, I try to remove the variable of being a "people person" from that equation. I think that it is important to lead by example and I think it's important to inspire others instead of motivating others. I think this is just as contrary as thinking leaders should not set high expectations. I don't think leaders are able to motivate others. I believe only individuals can motivate themselves. I don't think there is anything I can do to motivate others.

Our previous school superintendent was very charismatic. He was often asked to motivate the staff in several schools. He always said there was nothing he could do to motivate staff—they must motivate themselves.

As leaders, it goes back to identifying the unique individual characteristics of the people we lead. What inspires some may not inspire everyone. It takes tremendous effort to identify those characteristics, triggers and buttons to push. I think that's what leaders need to do.

Wright

In your career you've been responsible for decisions affecting the lives of thousands. Can you take us through your decision-making process?

Hub

One of the things I am most proud of is taking thirty-nine soldiers from Ft. Riley, Kansas in 1991 to fight a war in the Middle East and later that summer bringing thirty-nine soldiers back. On the front lines of Desert Storm, I constantly had to make decisions that profoundly affected lives in the moment. In the now, right then, lives were instantly affected by my decisions.

I think a hallmark of my decision-making process has been my integrity. As a young platoon leader, I stressed "deeds, not words." It's nice to say things about decision-making; it's nice to say things about leadership; it's nice to say things about management and decision-making, but doing is better than saying.

I define integrity as when your actions match your words. I think by having high integrity, leaders develop the ability to make decisions and they achieve the buy-in that is crucial for successful implementation.

I think that leaders who embrace consensus as a decision-making factor are doomed to failure. Making decisions through consensus-building is a temporary fad that I think is beginning to fade. Consensus-building takes forever and it must be reinforced daily. I think that using clear and direct communication, allowing patterns of decision-making to emerge, and encouraging dissents when making decisions is the best decision-making process leaders can use.

Lastly, David, I think that effective leaders in the twenty-first century know how to make the second best decision today rather than the best decision later.

Wright

I think a personal example regarding my strengths and decision-making is that I do not know geography well, and I don't follow politics, so I don't want to make decisions based on what happens and who we go to war with. I just hope that the people in those top positions can make those decisions.

Hub

I appreciate your articulation about the strengths prospective and my decision-making philosophy—that was an excellent example.

Jim Collins, in his classic book, *Good to Great,* talks about the "hedgehog concept." He advocates embracing what we can be our very best at doing. The very best leaders follow this guidance and it manifests itself most clearly when they say no—when they refuse to do something when it does not match their organization's mission and vision, and when it does not align with what the organization does best.

Often, leaders' plates overflow because they are not able to make the decision to say no. Saying no is not disrespectful. As a matter of fact, I think it's just the opposite—I think it's very respectful. I think effective leaders should suggest alternatives that might help solve the problem at hand. The ability to say no is powerful. What's even better is the ability to say no, but to come up with a solution tied into what the company does best—its strengths.

Wright

You have said that you don't think leaders should delegate tasks. I am eager to hear how they can get anything accomplished when they don't delegate tasks.

Hub

You know David, I just finished saying that as leaders, our plates "runneth over," and how in the world can we get anything done if leaders don't delegate tasks? My contrary views on leadership often frustrate others. I am very excited when I can keep everybody in the room during a speaking engagement after I clarify my stance on delegation.

I worked for a principal once who was notorious for delegating just about everything that came across his desk. He got a pretty bad rap for that. His reputation was that he didn't do anything—that he let his assistant principals run the school.

One specific example was selecting a keynote speaker for the eighth grade graduation program. The head high school principal should do that and always had. The eighth graders and their families in the crowd want to hear from their leader—the principal of their high school—the one they're going to see at the end of the summertime. The principal I worked for said he would not give the keynote address and he asked me to do it. Did he delegate that important task to me, or did he empower me to grow as a leader?

I challenge the people I speak with about leadership to do one very simple thing: remove the word "delegate" from their vocabulary and replace it with the word "empower." I think we would all agree that the end result is not going to change, but the recipient feels so much better when he or she is empowered to do a task instead of being delegated to do the task.

In summary, the principal I worked for empowered me to develop as a leader by giving me opportunity after opportunity. I'm clearly where I am today because I was given so many opportunities by my principal. This story takes us back to the very first topic we talked about—my passion and my persistence in developing others. It is so important for effective leadership and empowering others is the key to doing it well.

Wright

Not to mention the fact that he was building your leadership skills. As you were telling that story, what occurred to me was that those people who were listening to you looked at you very differently. He allowed you to get their trust. Your credibility was established.

Hub

I'm glad you picked up on that. Only leaders who are secure in their position, in themselves, in their skills, and in their individuality are able to give up power to others.

The freshman class was going to consider me the head principal. I was the one they had heard on graduation night. I was the one who had spoken to them and their parents. I was the one who drank Kool-Aid and ate cookies with them after the graduation ceremony. When they entered our high school with fifteen hundred other students, I was the familiar face. Immediately, just as you said, I developed a level of credibility with those students and those parents in that ninth grade community that I would have not have had otherwise. This very secure principal was not in the least insecure about that.

Wright

So what can be done to provide aspiring leaders the opportunities to gain skills necessary for leadership?

Hub

In the introduction it is stated that my personal vision is to have the greatest impact possible on the growth and development of others. That is what I'm about. That's what I want to be the very best in the world at. Anything I can do to grow and impact and influence and develop others is what I'm going to do.

In the corporate world we have seen the role of the Chief Operating Officer—the assistant, the number two person—dramatically change. I've also sensed this change happening in the non-profit and educational arenas. Someone is no longer the number two because they don't have the capability, the qualifications, and the characteristics to be the number one. Successful organizations today know that they must have a broad array of strengths in their number two positions. Leaders cannot do it themselves. The role of the number two person is crucial.

"Assistance for Assistants" is a high quality professional development program that I developed. It's designed specifically for current and aspiring leaders. We focus on continuous growth, constant feedback, and a strengths performance coaching perspective. (I always refer back to building strengths, not fixing weaknesses.) It's filled with measurable objectives and action plans tied to standards of professional development. It was developed as a strategic balance of leadership and management, with an eye on the emerging role of the number two. With this program we help participants develop their personal and leadership competencies. We also focus on the skills necessary to be emotionally and socially intelligent leaders in the 21st century. Workshop sessions in this program address specific challenges facing today's leaders. Typically a four-part series, it is standards-based and results-driven.

I talked before about continuous growth. I imagine all the authors in this book agree that continuous growth and sustained personal and professional development yield the greatest results and the greatest return on investment.

The high quality, professional development I deliver asks guiding questions such as: Why are relationships important to success? How can I become a better listener? Why do I need to equip and empower others? How does attitude impact leadership? How should I prioritize my life? How can I extend my influence? I think it's crucial to provide opportunities, and what's unique about this program is that it's designed specifically for those in that number two role. "Assistance for Assistants" is about how to be a great number two.

Wright

It sounds exciting. What a great conversation, Kevin. I really appreciate all this time you've taken with me to answer all these questions. You've given me a lot to think about and I know people reading this chapter will feel the same way.

Hub

Thank you for the opportunity.

Dr. Kevin F. Hub

Wright

Today we've been talking with Dr. Kevin F. Hub. His personal vision is to have the greatest impact possible on the growth and development of others. After listening to him today, I tend to believe he is going to be successful in that quest. He specializes in the personal development of current and aspiring leaders and we all know that's necessary for leading the way to success.

Kevin, thank you so much for being with us today on *Leading the Way to Success.*

Hub

Thank You.

About the Author

Dr. Kevin F. Hub is an Assistant Superintendent for Madison County Schools in Richmond, Kentucky, where he serves as Director of Human Resources. He also facilitates the "Grow Your Own" leadership cadre with more than one hundred members from Madison and other surrounding counties. He taught math and geography at Madison Central High School where he also worked as the school's Vice Principal. Kevin teaches graduate courses as an adjunct instructor in the Department of Leadership and Counseling and the Department of Curriculum and Instruction at Eastern Kentucky University.

He has presented at the state and national levels on various leadership topics, and has completed his Doctorate in Leadership Education from Spalding University in Louisville, Kentucky, where his dissertation work examined Emotional Intelligence Competencies of School Superintendents.

Dr. Hub is a graduate of the United States Military Academy at West Point, and served with distinction on the front lines in Desert Storm as an Infantry Officer in the United States Army.

Kevin lives in Richmond with his wife and three children.

Dr. Kevin F. Hub
HUB Consulting
1054 Center Drive, Suite #4
Richmond, KY 40475
859.893.3043 or 859.623.4740 (leave message)
Fax: 859.623.4741
Kevin@kevinhub.com
www.kevinhub.com

Dr. Kevin F. Hub

Chapter 4

Peter Sherer

THE INTERVIEW

David Wright (Wright)

Today we're talking with Peter Sherer.

Peter, welcome to *Leading the Way to Success*.

Tell us a little about your company, Experience Matters.

Peter Sherer (Sherer)

I started Experience Matters three years ago to help senior executives and professionals transition into a new job or the first stage of retirement. Since then I have worked with over two hundred and fifty senior people in the private sector, national non-profit organizations, and state and federal government agencies.

I believe that keeping Baby Boomer executive talent engaged in work that they love, is both what they say they need in survey after survey, and is crucial to maintaining institutions that make this country work.

Wright

You have been thinking about executive leadership and excellence for a long time. What do you see as the big picture in executive talent today?

Sherer

Executive Leadership is in short supply, and the demographics are going to make executive talent even scarcer for a whole generation. Retirement of

Baby Boomer leaders is a challenge to all the sectors, the private sector, the non-profits, and government at all levels. Governments are especially hard hit because the average age of the workforce is significantly older. That means there is a lot of experience in place now and an immediate need to retain that experience for as long as possible.

The retirement of Baby Boomers in great numbers is exacerbated by the smaller size of the workforce in the next generation, most often called Generation X. There are seventy-eight million Boomers but only half as many in the twenty-year cohort immediately following. That means every organization in the country is going to face a major challenge to recruit and retain experienced leadership. In fact, the Labor Department estimates that in two years there will be ten million unfilled professional jobs every year and that that number will grow to be thirty million jobs annually in just ten years.

Another aspect of the big picture is that it is a global phenomenon, particularly in the industrialized countries. We are heading into an international talent war. It is international because demographically the United States is younger than Europe and Europe is younger than Japan. That means that there will be continuing pressure by the Japanese and the Europeans to recruit American executive talent that we can hardly afford to lose.

For our part, we will make every effort to attract executive immigrants to make up the talent gap. This will be far easier for the United States to do, given our national mythology about being a melting pot, than it will be for Europe or Japan.

I asked a newly minted U.S. citizen who was born in Korea to tell me his nationality. Without hesitation, he said, "I am an American." I also asked a Japanese business executive friend of mine how long I would have to work in Japan before I was considered Japanese. Without missing a beat, he said, "Never."

Every industrialized nation is going to have to encourage executive immigration to maintain national productivity and it will be harder culturally for some than others.

Wright

As a career and retirement coach for senior executives, you are working with executives in all the sectors, but you are devoting a lot of your time these days on senior people in federal public service. Will you tell us why you are focusing there?

Sherer

Seventy percent of senior executives heading federal government agencies are eligible to retire in just two years. These are the people who keep our drinking water safe, issue social security checks, manage our national security, and carry out every law passed by the Congress.

That means we will have to retain and redeploy our executive talent to maintain continuity of services. The value of public sector career leadership is not well understood by the general public or in some cases by the leadership of the Executive Branch. But it takes a lot of management talent to make sure everyone gets the right social security check on time. It is now done so well that it is not an issue in the press or public discourse, but it will be.

After Katrina, we all saw the consequence of ill-prepared federal leadership. For the next twenty-five years, the issue will not be just a few poorly chosen political appointees because if we are not strategic now, the pool of emerging career executive talent will be too small and too inexperienced to succeed.

Personally, I understand how talented public sector executives are and how useful they can be after their first career. I get this both from my own public sector management experience and from watching my father's distinguished career as a high ranking Foreign Service Officer.

Wright

Will you give us some context by describing the leadership challenges facing senior executives in the federal government today?

Sherer

There are many, including keeping up with the possibilities of technology, increased national security needs, re-establishing trust with the American people, twenty years of shrinking agency budgets—particularly in the discretionary accounts of the domestic departments like Labor, HHS, and Education. Budget pressures will continue into the foreseeable future as we try to fight two wars, manage the credit crisis and cope with the costs of replacing our outdated infrastructure. But my biggest concern is in the human capital area. That means recruiting the right people into the right jobs and retaining them in federal service.

This won't be easy. The government is notoriously slow in its hiring practices. To be fair, part of the issue is the need to honor civil service requirements to hire career people based on merit rather than their political connections.

Nevertheless, on average, according to a 2002 Government Accountability Office report, it takes more than three months to hire a new employee. Often, the process extends over six months, and if a recruit needs a security clearance, it can take over a year. Meanwhile, talented prospective employees are getting offers from the private and non-profit sectors in a much shorter time frame.

In addition, the federal government has spent less on executive development every year for over two decades. That means that this much smaller cohort of emerging Generation X leaders are both less experienced and less well trained.

None of these issues is insurmountable, but they are going to require imagination, flexibility, and courage by government career leaders to change twenty-five-year-old talent acquisition and retention habits.

It's also going to require a leader bold enough to make the case that investing in people is essential and that the longer-term view demands it.

Wright

You said that the biggest challenge was to attract and retain scarce executive talent to public service. Will you say something more about the federal leadership necessary to meet this challenge?

Sherer

I just completed a survey of senior executive federal executives and I asked them why they were staying in their jobs, often past their retirement eligibility dates. Thirty-three percent reported that their jobs were very meaningful. Almost 40 percent reported that they were eager for a new assignment late in their career. In my mind, the surest way to insure retaining someone in an organization is to make sure that they "fit" with their job and that their interests and skills match the requirements of the job. Happy employees don't walk.

Most federal executives are never asked about whether they want to move to another slot where they might make an even more meaningful contribution. The old assumption is that people at this level are not eager for change, and that is simply not true. As a result, Uncle Sam has been losing valuable executive talent unnecessarily. People have retired because they outgrew their last assignment without being offered any alternatives.

The survey also indicated that most executives want a short sabbatical and another senior job in the government in a different part of their own agency or another government department. They have a feeling that "they have been there and done that." There is an opportunity to help them land in one more satisfying job, thereby delaying their departure for three to five years.

There is a whole different set of issues that need imaginative leadership if the government is going to create a hospitable environment for private or non-profit sector executives who want to work for the government after the end of their first career. These people heard JFK say that they should "ask not what their country should do for them but what they could do for their country" before they went off to their first careers. After the responsibilities toward children and mortgages have been met, many private sector executives respond to surveys saying that they want to "give back" by sharing their executive expertise.

This will be a challenging area. The cultures between the private sector and the public sector are very different. The private sector people have experience in working toward quarterly profit goals and are interested in boosting equity. Most government executives are pursuing social goals that are often less measurable in the short run. Authority in the private sector is pushed as far down the management chain as possible, where in government, the reverse is usually true. A President and his Cabinet often hold authority at a very high level to insure that their policies become implemented. This means a very long, and to some private sector executives, it would seem like a never-ending chain of authority before a decision can be made. A solid government-wide executive orientation is necessary including an explanation of the rationale underlying some key government procedures if the private sector to public sector migration is going to be successful.

Interestingly, there is an experiment underway now in which IBM is working to place some of its retiring executives in the Treasury Department. The process is being managed by The Partnership for Public Service, IBM, and the Treasury Department and is receiving financial support from the Atlantic Philanthropies Foundation. It is still very early in the experiment, but it is a worthy example of the kind of bold and imaginative leadership that is so badly needed now.

Wright

What people or organizations are making the biggest contribution to insuring continuity of senior federal leadership?

Sherer

Fortunately, there are an increasing number of groups that are beginning to get some traction with leaders in the executive and legislative branches. The National Academy of Public Administration, The Partnership for Public Service, The Council for Excellence in Government, and the IBM Center for the Business of Government are all important players in governmental systems improvement. However, my own view is that they have had a hard time raising the visibility of human capital issues because of serious competition within other issues like national security, health care reform, fiscal policy, and the capacity of the United States to improve conditions in the developing world. All these are extremely important, but my concern is who is going to be available to lead these efforts?

The responsibility for leading federal government-wide personnel management falls to the Office of Personnel Management. Many of the people who are supposed to worry about executive resources are retiring themselves and are very few in number.

Additionally, some of the collective inability to respond to this looming leadership crisis is because for the last thirty years, employers in all sectors were in a "buyers market." Every organization could just sort through the huge Boomer cohort until they found someone who met their needs. If that person didn't work out, they just found someone else who was eager to take that spot. Now, that is going to be impossible. The next twenty-five years are going to see an increasing shift to a "seller's market." With so few possible employees in the emerging leadership prospect pool, the power will shift toward the individual and away from the organization.

So the days of plentiful executive talent are over and many leaders are still operating on badly outdated assumptions. In five years, this issue will be declared a national emergency and there will be a rush of people who will say that Cassandra-like they were ignored. I will be dry-eyed about their leadership in this area unless they start to make a louder noise now.

Wright

What would you say were the leadership strengths of this group of executives, including some of the people you have coached?

Sherer

The first real strength of federal executives is their ability to handle issues with national and international scope. Their management experience is very broad because they often manage billions of dollars and tens of thousands of employees.

Another major skill is very sophisticated environmental scanning. Most major public sector initiatives have to create meaningful incentives for the private sector, other government agencies, and non-profits to become willing partners. This is even more complex, working on global initiatives. Often the task is intrinsically difficult to implement and evaluate in a timely manner. This is especially true when the goal is to change individual behavior, such as discouraging smoking or encouraging thrift.

To be an effective federal executive means having deep experience and expertise in a functional discipline, people skills, leadership ability, change management savvy, an ability to learn and adapt, communication know-how, a wide professional network, and track record of generating solid results. I am continually impressed by the breadth of the capacity and commitment of my clients.

Wright

As a coach, will you describe some of the issues that these executives are facing personally at this late stage in their first career?

Sherer

They are facing many of the same issues facing all the leading edge Baby Boomer executives in every sector and a few that are peculiarly the result of their public service history.

The major issue is what to do next that is worthwhile and has meaning. These people came to Washington after JFK's "Ask Not" speech and they have accepted modest pay, complicated bureaucratic rules, and uneven political leadership, all because they believed in their issue whether it was national defense, the environment, health, education, or international trade relations.

In general, Baby Boomers who wanted celebrity went to Hollywood, people who wanted money went to New York, and the people who insisted that their efforts contribute to the general welfare came to Washington, D.C. In my survey of senior executives, they reported that they have continued to stay for financial reasons, because they love their jobs, and because many of them don't know what to do next. They are physically and emotionally exhausted and they want to take a short sabbatical of up to one hundred and twenty days to think about the next steps. Many say that they want to return to government but in a new job in which they can both learn new things and apply their executive experience.

The difficulty for most federal executives is that they have lost sight of what they want to do because they have been too busy with their work and paying the bills. My contribution for the last several years has been to help individuals reconnect with the characteristics of a job that they would love. Uncle Sam could keep a lot of executive experience from leaving too early if political and career leaders took the time to treat people as individuals rather than part of a large group of potential retirees.

Specifically, senior executives are thinking about their possibilities in three distinct dimensions:

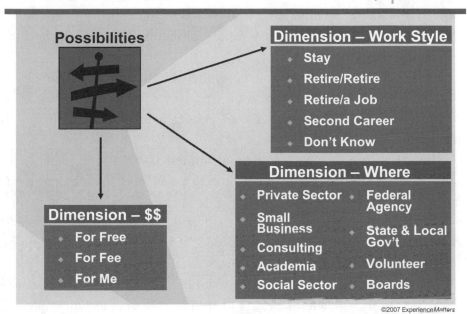

©2007 Experience*Matters*

The first issue is work style. Should they stay in the government, retire to a job, start a second career, or just retire to a quiet life? My clients have tried each of these strategies and the only ones who have run into trouble are the ones who think they can play golf as their main pursuit. Most find that there is not enough meaning in lowering their handicap and they then want to return to some sort of meaningful work.

The second concern is money. Some clients have enough money so they can afford to volunteer their time. Others want to generate a fee for their service in their own small business. Still others want to pursue an advanced degree or learn to play the violin to satisfy some long delayed passion.

For those who want to work, there is the issue of what sector would provide the most opportunity and fulfillment. Given the talent shortage, every sector will be looking for eager recruits.

Wright

Will you say something about what Baby Boomer executives are telling you about their plans for the next stage of life beyond their first career?

Sherer

Everyone has a six-month to-do list of deferred chores and fun things to do. They want to do things such as see the grandchildren, visit Machu Picchu, paint the house, play a favorite golf course in Scotland, and then get back to work.

Almost all the people who see me as they are thinking about life beyond their first career tell me that they want a part-time job that they love as part of a portfolio of other activities. Love means a job that is both fun and meaningful.

They also want to spend more time with their families and friends, more time to maintain their health, more time to travel, and some quiet time for spiritual pursuits.

Part-time work is a way to get paid and thereby handle the fear of outliving their money. It also keeps people in contact with like-minded others and is a measure of their worth.

The portfolio they are looking to create includes some balance between work, family, their health, friends, and spiritual pursuits including life-long learning. There is a keen interest in looking down a few of the roads not traveled up to this life stage.

Wright

What advice can you give to a reader who is trying to decide for him or herself about what to do in this third stage?

Sherer

The most important thing to do is to give yourself some time to take stock about the things that will be most important to you do during these next two or three bonus decades you have been given after your first career.

I have developed a series of eleven assessment tools to guide people through a productive introspection process. The first step is to understand the five or so key personal motivators that need to be in place in a work or volunteer situation for someone to flourish. I have created a list of thirty-three different personal motivators and I ask people to pick their top five favorite motivators. These can range from leadership to creativity to making a difference to spirituality and mentoring among others.

Then, given the importance of work, I encourage people to get in touch with the characteristics of a job that they would consider ideal. This is the same sort of analytical work that many have depended on in their professional careers but never thought to apply to deciding ideal personal next steps.

A good place to start is with subject matter. I say that if you adore going on long bike trips, what about documenting new bike trails for the National Park Service? If you are fascinated by genealogy, what about creating a company to help others trace their family histories? If you have always enjoyed mentoring, you might want to join the Peace Corps or teach a course at a junior college. If you love cars, how would you like to learn to be a mechanic? Choosing what is right for you begins with zeroing in on your passion.

The next step is to examine various jobs you have had and determine when you got so turned on—so in "the flow," that you lost track of time. What were you doing? Were you writing something important alone in your office or were you standing in front of a large group giving a speech? Were you happiest when you were representing your organization to another group or when you were quietly thinking about how to change the culture in your office? Sometimes we find our passion in volunteer jobs. Which volunteer assignments attracted you and what role did you play? If you've been green longer than Kermit the frog and love the outdoors, then you might consider teaching people to kayak or helping an organization clean up a river.

What about your role? Do you enjoy being the leader of an activity or would you prefer being a support troop? Leadership is so natural for some people that it is hard for them to be a team player. Others, however, don't want the responsibility or inevitable challenges of managing other people. What is the scope of the issue you might like to tackle—local, regional, national, or international? There are no rules, but you must decide for yourself what makes the most sense to you by carefully examining your head and heart.

The next issue is money and benefits. Some Boomers with young children may need major benefits. Other Boomers with defined benefit pensions might want to pick up some extra cash at a part-time job. And still others may dream of supplementing their grandchildren's college funds or reserving the outside cabin on a cruise.

Many Boomers are hoping to generate income for the first five to ten years after their first career, but exactly how much they require depends on their individual needs. I tell them that the important thing here is that they *do not* and I repeat *do not* think that they are doomed to limit their possibilities to what looks "practical." Most jobs will be created around willing and appropriate applicants.

When you have a sense of your ideal job, the next step is to find out where your ideal job exists. That means talking to people who have information about the intriguing new world you are seeking. The first stage in successful networking is to remind yourself of all the groups you have available. Many people do not think beyond their most obvious networks: colleagues at their current job, their family, and friends from their church, synagogue, or mosque. Anxiety sets in as they begin to worry that they don't know anyone who has the first idea about the area they want to investigate. They end their search before they have begun.

I advise my coaching clients to take ten minutes to identify at least fifteen different networks of people they can call upon to create an initial list of folks to see for advice. I remind them that they have an army of support, but they have just forgotten how many different people are available. These include college and graduate school alumni, neighbors, and personal service providers such as their doctor and dentist to name just a few.

With your list of networks in hand, you are ready to do a little reality testing by conducting informational interviews.

To illustrate the informational interview process, I am going to share a piece of my own story. In 1988, I was the Deputy Director of the President's Commission on Executive Exchange in the White House. The goal of the exchange was for public and private sector executives to appreciate the opportunities and constraints faced by their colleagues in the other sector.

My assignment was to find one-year jobs in the private sector for twenty federal Senior Executive Service members. In exchange, twenty private sector executives came to Washington to work as special assistants to Cabinet Secretaries. I loved helping these executives clarify what would be both exciting and career enhancing after their exchange year. I was proud of my work and the organization grew impressively.

With a change in the Administration, however, I had ninety days to find a new assignment. So I asked myself the same ideal job questions I recommended to my clients, and discovered that I was very interested in three issues: helping the homeless, improving secondary school education, and working in HIV/AIDS.

My next step was to talk with people in those fields to learn where I could contribute my skills at the salary level I needed to support my wife and then seventeen-year-old son.

I began by investigating the homeless field. A friend was running a national homeless organization and I asked for twenty minutes of her time over coffee. I explained what I was looking for and she told me that at my salary level, I would need a position that influenced national housing policy. At that time, she advised, national housing policy was being made by the tax committees on Capitol Hill. She suggested I speak with a staffer on the Hill from whom I learned that a law degree was the necessary passport to the right job there. This was critical information, because I already had an MBA and I could not afford to go to law school. So I shelved the homeless field.

Next, I began exploring elementary school improvement. Like most people, I was disheartened by the growing number of young children who couldn't read. I asked a teacher friend from church to suggest the names of people who were making national education policy. She recommended her college roommate who was working at the Department of Education. Her roommate agreed to have lunch with me. During that informational interview, I learned that to land the type of job I wanted, and to make any significant headway in the education field, I would need a PhD. With no time or money to work on a PhD, I started looking into the world of HIV/AIDS. I called an old graduate school colleague at the Public Health Service who referred me to the head of their National AIDS program office.

The doctor in charge referred me to a friend of his at the United Way, who referred me to the Executive Director of Washington, D.C.'s largest AIDS organization. He suggested that I see Richard Dunne, the wonderful man running New York City's largest AIDS organization, the Gay Men's Health Crisis. Richard told me that he had been approached to join the board of a brand new national HIV/AIDS organization funded by the Ford Foundation that was going to be headquartered in D.C, and he gave me the name of the new Executive Director.

Finally, I hit pay dirt. I contacted Paula Van Ness, the Executive Director of the new organization that was then called The National Community AIDS Partnership, and we hit if off famously. She hired me and over the next seven happy years, I raised $25 million for AIDS prevention and education in thirty-seven communities around the country. Over time, I helped grow the new organization into the National AIDS Fund. All my homework had paid off—it was a perfect match.

The major concept here is that informational interviews are not job interviews. The purpose of informational interviews is to find out more about possibilities in your area of interest, to meet the people who are important in that field, and to discover where a job with your ideal characteristics might be found. Informational interviews, unlike job interviews, are a very low risk way to ask all the questions that matter to you. The information you gather is the foundation for finding that job you will love, and very importantly, a way to avoid taking an assignment before you understand whether it is a good fit.

Wright

What are the opportunities of this "third stage of life" that you are describing?

Sherer

The biggest opportunity is to be in charge of your time. This is really the first time for many executives where they get to think creatively about the holy grail of a "balanced life."

In the early stages of a career, most executives are juggling their kid's soccer, elderly parents, sixty-hour workweeks, going to the grocery store, getting the car inspected, volunteering, shopping for the millionth household need, trying to schedule a dinner with friends, going to the gym, checking their PDA, finding two hours to read, do yoga, and go to the movies. It's tiring just reading this familiar list. And, according to many doctors, for twenty to thirty years, most of us go through life sleep-deprived. So, how do you balance your life during your working and child-rearing years?

My sad conclusion is that in mid-life life balance comes fleetingly, if at all. Don't despair, I tell my clients, it just comes with the territory. The answer during this hectic period is to craft as many quiet moments at the beach or the mountains as possible. Giving up the idea that there is a "right way" to balance your life is the beginning of sanity during this frenetic stage of life.

Often, when people get to their mid to late fifties, the kids are usually but not always gone and the house is no longer a burden. So freedom to fashion a life of one's own choosing is available for the first time. I tell my clients that there are a few useful things to remember about life after your first career:

Rule number one: What you give you can also take away. Anytime that something you are doing doesn't seem fulfilling, just stop doing it. Sounds simple, but we have all been accustomed to doing things we are not fond of in the workplace. For the sake of the mortgage or college tuitions, we occasionally put up with unpleasant colleagues, missed important family events, or were simply bored by repetitive assignments. Remember that this is your time now, so learn to leave commitments that don't meet your expectations as quickly and as gracefully as possible.

Rule number two: Your life portfolio management skills will improve. Creating a satisfying structure for your life when there is no time clock is a skill. Like any other skill, it takes time to develop, and, with practice, you will improve.

I have a retired friend who sits down with his wife every New Years Day to decide when they will take vacation time together. That is the first thing that goes onto the new calendar, and they never accept consulting assignments that interfere with those important times.

The first year after your full-time career is likely to feel as though you are learning to ride a bike. You may fall off a time or two, but you'll get the hang of it. After all, getting up and going to your old job created a whole series of showering, eating, and transportation rituals. These habits may be hard to break at first. Your new habits will soon develop their own rhythm.

Rule number three: It's a long way to Tipperary. One of the truly amazing things about the Boomer experience is that we have twenty to forty years left after our first careers. That means you have time to design several portfolios—not just one. My hunch is that the initial design will have a commercial or moneymaking component for most of us. Later on you will likely be doing more volunteering and lifelong learning. There are going to be a lot of people in their 70s and 80s learning new languages, new musical instruments, creating art, writing books, and new ways to stay healthy. So don't panic if you can't cram all your ideas into the first year of your newly balanced life.

Rule number four: Value is in the eye of the participant and not thebeholder. There is no one to apologize to for your choices. Someone is bound to think that spending eight hours a week learning how to play the harpsichord is a sign of imbalance. March on, secure in the knowledge that there will be seventy-eight million versions of the balanced life appearing over the next twenty years.

Rule number five: Expect to be thrown off balance sometimes. Parents get ill and die. A child suddenly needs attention after becoming a grownup. Your own health may cause you to change your pace or some cherished plan. Understanding that your best-laid plans are vulnerable to unpredictable circumstances will give you resilience when they inevitably occur.

Another area that occurs to my clients is, "How do I know when it is time to leave my full-time career?" My short answer is, when you are clear about what you are moving to rather than just what you are leaving behind. Clarity comes from giving some thoughts to the following areas:

Financial Questions—can I afford to retire? Have I taken advantage of all the free financial retirement planning resources offered by my company or agency? This affordability issue is what financial planners are trained to help you answer. Most Boomers will continue to work at least part-time until they are between seventy and seventy-five for the money, to have engaging colleagues, and a sense of purpose. The key is to get solid financial advice and then prepare to be flexible.

Psychological Questions—am I ready to leave where I am? Do I have a clue about how I am going to feel during the transition? The psychological impact is greatest for people who have been in the same agency or company for a long time. Ask yourself, "Do I have the passion about something?" Hang in there, get some exercise, and see friends and family who are supportive. Do I have a passion about something I want to do or am I just bored? Many people aren't ready to leave their organization, but they "have been there and done that" with their assignment. Look around, see if there is something worth doing in your organization, and then start to look outside. Most retirees say that they would have liked one other assignment that was interesting before they left.

Social Questions—where do I want to live? Do I want to move to a new geographic location? What impact will that have on my family and my network of friends? The key issue here is whether you need to maintain contact with the community that has supported you for the last decade or two. For some people, the lure of the beach is stronger. For others, the thought of having no history with the people they meet in their new environment sounds lonely.

Physical Questions—what is my current health situation? Do I need a physical tune up? This is the time to make up for missed dentist appointments and that long put-off colonoscopy. Everyone says that the most important ingredient in a successful retirement is feeling well enough to enjoy it.

Spiritual Questions—will my choice give me sufficient meaning and purpose? How can I be engaged and not just active? This is a big deal for most Washington, D.C., based Boomers I coach. Many people will find the same sort of enthusiasm in the not-for-profit sector. The key is to choose an organization and a role that matters.

The next step is to take some action. You will have twenty-five or thirty years to do all the things that interest you, so the assignment is to figure out what you want to do first. The big picture message is that you can have it all, just not all at once.

Wright

What are the barriers that you see to executives finding assignments that allow them to continue to contribute at this stage?

Sherer

We are in the early years of a major change where Baby Boomer executives are going to be in the work force for fifteen to twenty years beyond the traditional retirement age. Most organizations are slow to realize that they need to hold on to their increasingly scarce senior resources. That means that they are much less flexible than executives need them to be at this stage of life. Flexible work, job-sharing, flexible benefits will all have to be in place for organizations to appeal to this crowd.

An example in the non-profit world is that the volunteer coordinator is usually a recent college graduate who is used to suggesting that Boomers either go on the Board to raise money or stuff envelopes. Boomers are going to want to do high level episodic consulting. They want to put in a new financial system and then go to Arizona for three months. Understanding the interests and capacity of senior professionals is a sophisticated enterprise. I predict that the non-profits elevating the salary and sophistication of the volunteer coordinator position and salary soon will attract the most volunteers who can affect the organization in a major way.

Ageism is a factor but not for long. Like everything else the Boomers touch, seniority will be cool. Words like *experience* and *wisdom* will be in vogue and grey hair will something to strut rather than cover up.

The biggest barrier is cultural. We don't think of living with brains, money, and health into our mid 80s. Both Boomers themselves, the organizations that they work for, and public policy are all going to have to catch up to this new reality. Pension laws and social security regulations will have to be changed from discouraging people to work beyond a certain age to encouraging their participation. It will happen very soon as the leading edge Boomers retire in sufficient number and start putting pressure on all these institutions as surely as they did when they caused the need to build huge numbers of new elementary schools.

Wright

As an executive coach, tell us a little about a recent client who made a successful transition.

Sherer

Most of my public service clients move successfully to other jobs within the government because after the assessment process, they know what will bring them meaning and satisfaction. Some choose to leave for personal reasons.

Charlotte Bryan comes to mind. On September 11, 2001, Charlotte Bryan was racing back up Interstate 95 to Washington to assist her colleagues at the Federal Aviation Administration, where she served as the Director of Airports in Civil Aviation Security. Once there, she served as the head of the operations center for the next thirty-five hours. In the days following the attacks, she and her colleague alternated command of the operations center while the other slept. She was asked things unimaginable a short time beforehand. A general from North American Aerospace Defense Command (NORAD) called Charlotte to ask whether he should launch fighter jets. Pilots from all over the world, including a Chinese pilot with a planeload of anxious passengers, stood by to hear her instructions on whether they had permission to enter U.S. airspace.

A few months later Charlotte came to me because she said that she needed to leave her post in the government because she wanted more time at home with her son who was in his last year of high school. We went through the assessments I described and Charlotte decided to start her own consulting firm. I am pleased to report that she is now very happily helping premier airports around the world improve their security procedures. She is great and just one of many.

A senior executive of a major international shipping firm is now a leader in The Innocence Project. A senior IRS lawyer is now very happily selling Mary Kay cosmetics. A trade association executive realized her lifelong ambition and is going to nursing school this fall. A senior Justice Department lawyer is now consulting to large non-profits. I could go on, but you get the point. Over the next decade or two, we will see seventy-eight million different stories and a general understanding that there is a whole new and exciting stage after completing a first career.

Wright

As a last question, when you speak to a cross section of private, public, and non-profit executives, what do you say are the key lessons have you learned from your recent work?

Sherer

I tell them that the quality of their management talent is the key success factor in their enterprise. I tell them to develop a culture where it is safe for senior people to tell them the date when they plan to retire so that real succession planning is possible

I emphasize that they should help people move into meaningful jobs with the organization until employees are well into their 70s.

I ask them to analyze their personnel policies and procedures to remove all the incentives that are in place for people to leave.

I remind them that understanding the needs of senior executives is a retail not a wholesale process. Asking people what they want and then accommodating their needs is the surest way to build loyalty beyond the traditional retirement years.

I conclude by telling them that they don't have much time to react and that this demographic phenomenon will be with them for the next twenty-five years.

I usually get enthusiastic applause at the end of my speeches, but only after a moment of stunned silence.

About the Author

Peter Sherer, founder and CEO of Experience Matters, is a nationally known strategic consultant and executive coach, improving the morale and effectiveness of both outstanding organizations and fast track senior executives.

Prior to becoming a consultant and coach, Sherer was an executive in both the public and non-profit sectors. He served as Deputy Director of the President's Commission on Executive Exchange, a White House initiative designed to increase understanding between the business and government sectors. Sherer helped senior executives in both the private and public sectors to switch with their counterparts into career enhancing one-year assignments. At the Department of Health and Human Services, he served as the project manager for the implementation of The Civil Service Reform Act covering 150,000 employees.

After college, Sherer was awarded a Rockefeller fellowship to the Harvard Divinity School. He then founded Project Place to serve runaway children in Boston, and went on to receive an MBA from the Harvard Business School with second-year honors.

He is a recognized author and sought-after speaker on career management and how organizations can increase productivity by retaining senior executives and their institutional wisdom. Sherer has coached over 250 public and private sector executives in career transition, performance improvement, and organizational restructuring. He serves as a member of the Senior Executive Association, a Principle of the Council for Excellence in Government, and is a certified coach for the Federal Consulting Group and is a graduate of Coach University.

He also has extensive experience as a senior executive in outstanding national non-profit organizations including a Ford Foundation initiative, the National AIDS Fund. At the National AIDS Fund, he was responsible for raising a total of $25 million as the first Director of Development and Communications. During his tenure, the Fund grew from serving eight cities to 37 cities with over 3,000 grants. While there, he recruited a national Board of Directors that included CEOs of Fortune 100 companies, international celebrities, and senior national foundation leaders.

Recently, Sherer has addressed groups ranging from the Central Intelligence Agency to the Council for Excellence in Government, the Performance Institute, the Smithsonian Associates and the Treasury Executive Institute.

Peter Sherer
Founder & CEO
***Experience*Matters**
21 Third Street NE
Washington DC
202-210-5587
www.expmatters.com

Peter Sherer

Chapter 5

Barbara Taylor & Jane Lowenstein

THE INTERVIEW

David Wright (Wright)

Today we're talking with Barbara Taylor and Jane Lowenstein, partners in JanBara & Associates.

Barbara has extensive experience working with senior leaders in large and mid sized corporations. She has designed and implemented effective War for Talent strategies for numerous Fortune 500 clients. Her expertise focuses on business coaching, talent management, and succession planning, leadership development, high potential identification, hiring selection and assessment, and performance management. Barbara has built a reputation for designing creative leadership development programs such as the Gettysburg Leadership Experience.

Jane has over twenty-five years experience advising corporate executives how to solve their people problems. Her clients have described her as a perspective and insightful coach who produces exceptional results. She has taught managers and executives how to develop and lead others to reach organizational goals, create an environment for high performance, and develop an adaptable, competent workforce to handle tough issues. Jane excels in strategic communications, facilitation, change management, diversity, and succession planning. As a federal mediator, she has extensive experience with conflict management and alternative dispute resolution techniques.

Jane and Barbara, and their associates, focus on the critical success factors that cause individuals and organizations to succeed. Addressing the development and retention of leaders, they create strategies and programs to ratchet up the performance of both organizations and individual leaders.

JanBara specializes in the issues of professional women in the business world, providing executive coaching, and leadership development. They have created leading edge workshops and group coaching programs for women around the effective use of power, influence, and impact and are known in the Philadelphia area for several successful series.

Barbara, Jane, welcome to *Leading the Way to Success*.

Barbara Taylor (Taylor)

We're glad to be here. Thank you, David

Wright

So, men and women deal with the same universal leadership issues, but there are some unique leadership situations that women face more predominately or more frequently. Would you share with our readers what these are?

Jane Lowenstein (Lowenstein)

The design for success was developed by men. When women do not behave in accordance with that definition, they are found lacking. Women can follow men's lead and alter the behavior they were raised with or they can pursue a more inclusive style of decision-making, problem-solving, communication, and leadership.

The problem is that men can see women's collaborative skills as evidence that we cannot make up our minds, we can't make decisions, or we lack confidence or even competence. Knowing when to project different leadership styles presents greater challenges for women.

In addition, men sometimes apply a tougher standard to women: "If you want to play in the game, you'd better be good!" This is all the more reason for women to be at the top of their game at all times. This can be difficult and hard to accomplish. Often, since women are the newer kids on the block, they may not be given the space and time to develop and to make mistakes. All of these things present greater challenges and perhaps unique leadership situations for women.

Wright

Women have always been in the workplace in "women's jobs," but in the last sixty-five years, especially since World War II, women have really taken their seat in some of the board rooms and especially in the workplace. Why are there still differences between men and women in the workplace?

Taylor

I'd like to push back slightly on something that you just said by using the adage, "The more things change, the more things stay the same." While there are more women in senior management and a number of women on corporate boards, the quantity is not significant. There's a non-profit organization in New York called Catalyst that does research about women in the workplace. What they have found is discouraging. Even in 2008, women's salaries are 80 percent of those of men. The number of women who are on track to go into the corner office has also dropped. Some of that may be because of downsizing in our economy right now.

However, an interesting fact is that while there are more women with MBAs, law degrees, and solid business experience than ever before, the number of women in senior positions or who have significant profit-loss responsibilities has not moved appreciably. Women are certainly considered professionals, but their advancement into companies' business areas has lagged behind. It is frustrating for women who are certainly getting the experience they would have hoped would have projected them into more visible areas of responsibility.

So, some things have changed, but some things have not. Additionally, the number of women who currently are on corporate boards is low—about 12 percent. Catalyst's research indicates that if the number of women being appointed to boards continues to go at the same rate as it is now, it will be over fifty years before there is parity between men and women in the boardroom. Jane eluded that the business environment was created by men. What happened is that the definition of what are "successful behaviors" (those behaviors that propel people to success) were fashioned from behaviors that men used.

71

Women have many of the same "success" attributes and behaviors as men. For instance, women and men both have high performance standards; both have dedication to jobs and will work the necessary long hours to meet high-level goals. But women, probably through genetics (our brain works differently) and social mores, do not react the same as men do in certain situations. We are more collaborative, so when we go in to talk to our staff and to our superiors, we tend to try to get more input than a man might.

Women, by the way, can also lack some perceived overt executive presence, sometimes due to size itself. When we walk into a room, we might not necessarily have the commanding presence that a man might have. Women don't always have some of the characteristics that make us seem as if we are "leaders."

The last thing I'm going to mention is that our communication styles are different. Jane will go into a little bit more about this. So, those are some of the reasons why there are differences between men and women in the workplace.

Wright

So why is there such a disparity between men and women in terms of salary?

Lowenstein

Women often accept the salary a new employer offers. They do not as readily negotiate for an increase. Men are much more likely to negotiate for a higher amount. In fact, research shows that if a woman accepts $5,000 less as a beginning salary, at the end of her work life, she will have earned $1.5 million less.

For example, I was hired for a position at a lower level than a man, even though we were equal in experience and education, because the assumption was made that he had a family to support. He didn't—they just made that assumption. So if this had not been corrected, I would have forever been making less money than Sam.

Wright

But why would that have made any difference even if it were true? So he had a family to support, what difference does that make?

Lowenstein

It doesn't make a difference, but my employer made an assumption that he would need more money because he had more mouths to feed.

Taylor

And you're also right, David, that whether he did or didn't, or whether Jane did or didn't, it's not the issue. The issue is that there should be equal pay for equal work.

Wright

I have about thirteen females working for me and every one of them is the wage earner—the highest wage earner—in their family.

Taylor

Exactly, especially in more contemporary times, as more women have come to work, more women are the primary wage earner in their family. Making those old assumptions can be very detrimental to women. And, since pay increases are determined on base salaries, if a woman started out making less, she will continue to stay behind the eight ball.

Wright

So why is there such a disparity between men and women in senior management, etc.?

Lowenstein

Part of the reason for the scarcity of women in senior management is that women don't apply for jobs unless they feel they have already developed the competencies needed to do the job. Men apply for jobs that look interesting or will provide them the opportunity to work in a new part of the business or for jobs where they will be placed in a position for greater advancement.

We have coached a woman at a large bank. She watched her colleagues climb the corporate ladder faster than she did because she did not apply for jobs unless she felt she deserved them. If women persist in this approach, they will continue to lag behind men in rising to senior positions.

In addition, women don't always exhibit the same behavior as men in terms of decision-making, problem-solving, or communicating. Women are concerned about how others will be affected by decisions. This is not to say that men are not, but studies show that this is more prevalent in the behavior and attitude of women in the workplace. Because men may interpret women's behavior as lacking decisiveness or lacking ability, women may not be promoted at the same rate as men or given the same developmental assignments. Since women are the "newcomers" to the corporate environment and their inclusive style is seen as weakness, not as many make it to the senior echelons.

Also, men need to make room for what women have to offer. At any level, a diversity of opinion, perspective, and experience is a good thing. Leaders need to make room for women in the operating functions of organizations, not in just the staff or advisory functions.

Wright

Do women develop leadership skills differently than men?

Taylor

They do develop differently because of what is open to each gender. There are three main ways that people actually increase their capability and competency:

- Through varied work experience
- Through people—including bosses (good and even bad bosses), mentors, parents, teachers, etc.
- Through coursework, seminars, etc.

Of the three above, work experience is by far the most powerful and fosters the most significant learning. Both men and women can learn from work challenges, work variety, and hardships. However, mostly men get the types of jobs that are very much *in* the business—the operations of the business. This, of itself, provides them with the types of experiences that can grow them to get into that corner office or to more senior level positions.

Women tend to get the jobs that *surround* the business—the service areas, the corporate functions such as HR or Community Involvement.

These are not the core business itself. So, when companies do their succession planning for their senior positions, they're going to promote their employees who have the "right" operational experience. Therefore, women have a disadvantage in this most important way to increase their capability and competency.

Jane and I coach women to go after these core jobs and responsibilities. It's the best way for women to even the playing field.

Lowenstein

In fact, I do want to relay what I think is a funny story, and it has to do with the political scene. A woman researcher was looking at why there are so few women in American politics. (Did you know that the United States has fewer women in politics than the government in Afghanistan? That's shocking.) So this female researcher interviewed quite an extensive number of men and women. Some of the questions she asked were, "Have you ever been asked to serve or run in something political? Have you either run for office or served on a big committee?" One woman replied, "No, not really," but in probing further with this woman, the interviewer found out that the mayor had asked her to be part of a very important task force. When the researcher said, "But here you are, really involved in that." The woman replied, "Oh that doesn't really mean anything. That's really not important."

Conversely, the researcher interviewed a man who when asked, has anyone ever requested you to run for office, replied, "Absolutely," In digging further, she found out that he had been to a bar, was having a few drinks, and was talking with the bartender This man had lots of opinions about the local political scene. So, the bartender said to him, "You know, you ought to run for office." So, this counted as a yes answer to being asked to run for office.

Now obviously, those are two extremes, but the reason we bring this up is because this is very much the model of what happens between men and women. Women tend to feel that we must have had the experience. We must have proven ourselves. We don't necessarily take risks as men do.

Wright

I just always assumed that men were in politics and women were not because women were more intelligent than men.

What does it mean that women are "caught in a double-bind"?

Taylor

The double-bind is "you're damned if you do and damned if you don't." That's basically the double-bind. What it means for women is that men and women have certain perceptions of how women should act. So, what happens in the business world is that if a woman acts below a certain standard, she's considered weak, too touchy-feely, too feminine, or too emotional. But, if a woman uses the same assertive behaviors a man would, she's labeled the notorious B word.

So, women have to walk a narrow path of behaviors where they're not too wimpy, but also considered not too aggressive. How do you actually balance that? That's the double-bind.

I'm going to give you an example that to me is pretty telling. Late last year, a woman was on the fast track to be the first CEO on Wall Street at Morgan Stanley. She was fired, and her name was Zoe Cruz. The CEO's name was John Mack, and the reason I mention their names is that each of them had nicknames. John Mack, the CEO, was given the name of "Mack the Knife." This was said in good humor and was considered a positive attribute in that it showed that Mack was sharp and incisive. Zoe Cruz was called "Cruz Missile." Now to me, "Cruz Missile" could be a pretty cool name as well—describing a person who was really targeted and hit her goals, etc. But in Zoe's case, "Cruz Missile" was considered negative. It was said in a way that was pejorative—that she wasn't acting the way that a woman should act, that she was being too assertive, taking on too much, and was not working into traditional social mores.

Wright

So, if a man and a woman exhibit the same behavior, the man is called aggressive and the woman is called a bitch?

Taylor

Yes, the very same behaviors can be identified differently depending on gender.

Wright

So, how do people react differently to men versus women in terms of displaying anger?

Lowenstein

In men, anger is seen as passion and commitment to accomplishing the goals. In women, it's seen as being overly emotional. Recent research presented at an Academy of Management Conference discovered that if men get angry, it is seen as a reasonable response to a tough situation. If women show anger, they're seen as weak and unable to control their emotions.

We have coached a woman who had a heated discussion with a male counterpart during a staff meeting. Her male counterpart was complimented for his dedication. She was called into her boss's office and counseled to keep her emotions under control.

We still have a long way to go before anger is seen as an acceptable response from a female.

Taylor

In fact, Jane, didn't that study also show that when a man loses his temper, he actually gains "points"?

Lowenstein

Yes, he can, whereas a woman loses points big time. In fact, she may not be considered an acceptable leader because she can't control her reactions.

Wright

So how can women be perceived as having leadership potential?

Lowenstein

In general, there are a number of behaviors that women need to pay attention to or develop. One of them is to start bragging. Women can often be uncomfortable talking about the good things that they have done. We need to ask for what we want and not just accept the status quo. We need to negotiate, speak up, and hold our ground when someone tries to interrupt us. When we're discussing a topic, begin with the point that we're trying to make. Then provide the supporting documentation. Because men prefer to hear the bottom line first with support for the conclusion following, women can be seen as indecisive if they can't get to the point quickly enough.

Women need to start thinking out of the box. In fact, forget the box, just try on unproven new ideas. Don't assume that good things like promotions will come to you if you just do a good job.

Barbara and I have found that sometimes younger women believe good things will happen if they just focus on doing a good job—recognition will come. That's not the way men act. Men go after what they want. They work *on* their jobs, not just *in* them.

Some other ideas for increasing women's leadership potential:

- If you get stopped, find a way around whatever obstacle is in your way.
- Take credit for what you've done.
- Recognize that being comfortable is overrated. Sometimes (often times) you need to fake it 'til you make it. You need to take actions you've not done before, even though it's uncomfortable. Do it anyway.
- If there's a big decision coming up at a meeting, talk to the decision-makers before the meeting. Get their opinions; explain your reasons for supporting the project, so there will be fewer surprises in the actual meeting. Barbara calls this "hallway management."
- Continue to bring your humanity to work.
- Make statements. Don't make requests in the form of questions unless you really need information.
- Propose solutions that you haven't tried before. It's the same principle as applying for a job. Don't only propose solutions you've already tried.
- Exhibit confidence, even if you're not feeling confident.
- Watch your posture and the tone and the pitch of your voice. Only 7 percent of our message is delivered through our words; 38 percent comes from our tone and 55 percent comes from our body language. If we raise the volume, speed, and pitch of our voices when we feel nervous, we might not sound like we're confidently in control and ready to take on the big challenges.

Wright

Why do so many people say they never want to work for a woman?

Taylor

You know, we hear this with some frequency, and it's painful. It's particularly painful when we hear women say that about other women. Basically, it deals with some of the things we've already talked about. The business environment was designed by men, and therefore, men's behaviors and attributes are used to describe positive leadership role models.

Both male and female direct reports and peers subconsciously become held by these standards. Both genders can react negatively when a woman manager does not conform to their belief of how women should act. Women expect other women to show warmth and understanding. If a woman manager is demanding, doesn't smile frequently, or doesn't wish to socialize about non-work subjects, her female direct reports may think she is acting "uppity" and is "too big for her shoes." If their male boss had the same behaviors, it wouldn't even be noticed.

Interestingly, male direct reports would feel something similar. They would find the above woman manager too aggressive but would not even think twice if a male manager exhibited the same behaviors.

Conversely, more men than women direct reports have problems with women managers who show more feminine leadership traits. Males may misconstrue their women managers' collaborative behavior or her seeking input as being wishy-washy, indecisive, and weak. Women tend to show their emotions more readily then men and this can cause discomfort.

Underlying the complaints about working for women are two issues:

- First, direct reports can be right—their woman boss may not be a good leader or manager. She may not have the appropriate leadership skills.
- Second, leadership is a diversity issue. There is no one right way to be a great leader. It is important for managers to be authentic, yet flexible. We certainly don't recommend women to be men, but we do advise our women clients to learn to flex their leadership approaches in certain situations. At the same

79

time, all men and women in business need to learn to be more flexible in how they are led.

Wright

When are a woman's collaborative skills viewed as lacking decisiveness or leadership capability?

Lowenstein

Women were raised to be communal—to consider the feelings and self-esteem of others in human interactions. So we have mannerisms that may not serve us well when men are evaluating us. For example, women often (and I do this myself) raise their hands in meetings when they want to speak. Men, on the other hand, believe that when they are speaking, they have the power. So they just jump right in.

Other behaviors that may not serve us well include:

- When we make requests in the form of questions, we might sound uncertain. For example, "Can you get me the data by Thursday?" instead of just saying," I need the information by Thursday."
- Often we won't talk about our accomplishments because it might make other people feel badly, so we defer taking credit for work well done. We need to take credit for the good work that we do. That's part of how leaders are evaluated—past performance predicts future accomplishments.
- Sometimes women don't ask for the resources they need to do a good job, they just do it themselves.
- Often, women use qualifiers, such as, "This may not be what you want to hear, but I've researched all the applicable sources, and the report reflects the current state of the law." A more powerful way to express that thought is, "I've researched all the applicable sources, and the report reflects the current state of the law."

These are examples of how women can sound more tenuous, less certain of our opinions, and less deserving of recognition. Leaders are not chosen from among the ranks of the unconvincing.

Taylor

And, building on what Jane was saying, women have this tendency that if there is a problem, they will ask for input from their staff or from peers, etc. This is a great collaborative skill, and it is what companies have been saying they want. But we have known and coached women who, because they have used these collaborative skills, are not considered leadership material. They're not thought to be decisive enough. The precise skills that companies say they want, when women use them, can hinder their careers. It's an interesting phenomenon.

Wright

So, what do you think are some general female traits that are conducive to today's business world?

Taylor

We've just covered a major one—collaboration and being a team player. Women's collaborative skills are absolutely conducive to globalization and working in the world economy.

Our communication skills are very in tune with globalization. We tend to be more expressive, ask for and provide more information, etc. Also, women tend to build solid relationships, which is what business is really about. Women have this innate ability to create good relationships. Additionally, women may have a slight edge on how to build a staff, looking at the competencies and skills their people need in order to have a very effective unit. These are the types of traits that women bring into the workplace.

Wright

I come from the University of Tennessee, where Pat Summitt is the girls' basketball team coach. She is probably one of the most revered women in the world, and she's certainly been a role model for many, many women. As you look at the WMBA now, it's almost the Pat Summit show.

So do mentors make a difference in a woman's career?

Lowenstein

Absolutely, and the example that you just gave is a perfect one. When you're in a mentoring relationship you get:

Barbara Taylor & Jane Lowenstein

- A role model
- A coach
- A person to listen to you with whom you can try out your ideas
- The ability to practice in a safe environment
- Feedback
- Introductions to others who can help your career
- Advice on which career path to follow
- A sounding board
- Advice on how to talk to people in different situations
- Someone committed to your development who pushes you to take responsibility for your career and performance and someone who motivates you to take those actions that will propel you to the accomplishment of your goals

We have found that mentors can be an invaluable resource for a woman's career.

Wright

You've said that networking skills are really important, so how do women's networking skills help or hinder them in business?

Taylor

On the surface, it looks like women's networking skills are better than men's, mostly because women wish to create relationships, and we generally have good communication skills.

David, I'm going to ask if you see a difference in this from your perspective as a man. For instance, Jane and I belong to a lot of networking groups, but it is hard for us, as we network to ask for business, to ask for a referral. Jane and I almost have to write it down on our palms to ask for a referral. Many women find this difficult also. David, do you find it difficult to ask for a referral?

Wright

Not at all.

82

Taylor

Most men react the same way. Women do have a problem with this, so the idea of networking and taking it to the final step is not something that women are always prepared for or feel comfortable doing. We tell ourselves, and others to just get over it, feel uncomfortable, push through it.

There was a study in the *Harvard Business Review* that Jane and I found fascinating. When superstar men and women left a company to go to another company, what they found is that the men superstars stalled in their next job. Women superstars did not. Now why did that happen? What the research found is that women did a better job of creating strong client relationships; so, when women moved, their clients went with them. The men didn't build that type of client loyalty in their relationships; so, when they moved, their clients generally didn't follow.

Conversely though, men develop better relationships inside their company, so they get to know the movers, the shakers, and the people who are really important for them to know as they build their careers. Men have mentors who can help them navigate the organization. Women don't tend to build these same strong internal relationships. The same relational avenues are not open to women. In today's world, it is still not uncommon for there to be meetings, outings (e.g., football games, etc.) where the men are asked to go but the women are not. So women may not build important internal networking paths and their careers can suffer for that.

Wright

Well, what a wonderful conversation. I really have enjoyed talking with both of you and I have learned a lot.

Lowenstein

I want to add one other thing. Women are leaving corporate America at a faster pace than men to start their own businesses. If we don't make room for women and for their types of "success" behaviors, we risk losing the great opportunity of what women have to offer.

Wright

As I checked your Web site, I see that JanBara & Associates has created some very interesting programs. Will you talk about a few of them?

Taylor

One of our most visible programs is Conversations with Women Leaders® (CWL). It is a multi-faceted leadership development program for women in the corporate world. Four times a year, women leaders and women on a career path to the top gather for a spirited CWL workshop. The goal at each half-day session is to come away with realistic action steps for career challenges, opportunities, and obstacles.

Women at higher levels face many situations they can't solve with abstract textbook theories or free-ranging office bull-sessions. The CWL sessions are designed to fill that gap.

Each session is moderated by us; we are experts at helping people find resolutions for workplace problems. The half day of activities includes time to describe individual challenges, interact with esteemed panelists, develop action strategies, and get to know the rest of the motivated participants.

Session attendees often say they find renewed enthusiasm for future challenges, while taking home practical tactics to use immediately.

Lowenstein

We also lead a program called the Sales Action Forum® (SAF) that focuses on facilitated discussion among sales and business development professionals. The participants have the opportunity to present their specific sales challenges and receive feedback, advice, and support from others in the group. Most groups have ten to twelve participants. Together, they develop action steps to change behaviors and attitudes that might be holding them back from achieving the sales they desire.

Additionally, we have a new program, Strategic Client Connections (SCC). We feel this program is incredibly valuable in our current economic environment.

We help our client companies become centers of influence for their own clientele

- By having them host a small group of their business connections for an intimate networking event and
- By deepening the relationships between their own staff and their clients (or potential clients)

The purpose of our highly focused SCC session is for a company's clients to get to know each other so they can grow their relationships and their businesses. This is not a "show and sell" proposition, but an opportunity for a company's current/prospective clients to share and learn from each other. Our belief is that the more people who know what a company does, the better their "word-of-mouth" marketing will be.

Wright

These are very, very interesting subjects. I really appreciate both of you taking so much time with me here today to answer all these questions. I think our readers are really going to have their eyes opened and learn from what you have said.

Lowenstein

David, it was our pleasure.

Taylor

Absolutely.

Wright

Today we've been talking with Jane Lowenstein and Barbara Taylor. Together they own JanBara & Associates. Jane excels in business coaching, leadership development, strategic communications, facilitation, change management, and diversity. As a federal mediator, she has extensive experience with conflict management and alternative dispute resolution techniques. Barbara's expertise focuses on business coaching, talent management, succession planning, leadership development, high potential identification, hiring, selection assessment, and performance management. So you can just imagine how they work well together.

Jane, Barbara, thank you so much for being with us today on *Leading the Way to Success*.

Taylor

Thank you, David.

Lowenstein

Thank you very much, David.

About the Authors

Barbara Taylor, offers 20+ years of expertise in business coaching; talent management and succession planning; leadership development; high potential identification and deployment; assessment; and performance management.

Barbara has built a reputation for designing creative leadership development programs including. The Gettysburg Leadership Experience and Group Coaching for Women & Power. She has designed and implemented effective War for Talent strategies for numerous Fortune 500 clients including Comcast, GlaxoSmithKline, Invesco, Infineum, AstraZeneca, L. Robert Kimball & Associates, and Sara Lee.

Currently, she and her business partner, Jane Lowenstein, lead JanBara & Associates, a coaching and executive development firm specializing in the issues of professional women in the business world. JanBara & Associates facilitates leadership development and coaching services for the East Coast clients of ASK Europe, a British learning and development organization. She is one of the innovators and facilitators of the Conversations with Women Leader Series designed for high potential and emerging business women to discuss issues, dilemmas and sticky business predicaments that can make or break careers. She has also developed Executive Woman Roundtables to meet the special needs of senior level women executives. Previously, Barbara worked for Lincoln Financial Group where she led Executive and Leadership Development strategies.

Certified in various leadership and organizational development approaches including 360 degree feedback, MBTI, DiSC and Situational Leadership. Barbara completed a Bachelor of Science in Communications at Ohio University. She is a member of the Board of Directors of Girls, Inc and Nancy's House as well as on the Career Wardrobe Advisory Board.

Barbara lives with her husband in a suburb near Philadelphia. She is an avid reader, dedicated to the restoration of their 112 year old Colonial Revival home and enjoys wearable art.

Jane Lowenstein is a partner in JanBara & Associates, an executive coaching, leadership development and consulting practice. Her clients describe her as a perceptive and insightful coach who produces exceptional results. For over 25 years, she has taught managers and executives how to lead others to reach organizational goals, solve people problems, create an environment for high performance and develop an adaptable, competent workforce to handle tough issues. She coaches executives and consults with organizations of varying sizes from GlaxoSmithKline, Invesco, Citizens Bank, Infineum, Comcast, L. Robert Kimball & Associates, and Sanofi Aventis to entrepreneurs in emerging businesses. Jane facilitates leadership development programs and provides coaching services for ASK Europe, a British learning and development organization and has conducted training and organizational assessments in businesses, schools, government institutions, universities, and non-profit organizations.

Having created the Conversations with Women Leaders series, Jane and Barbara facilitate discussions to address the particular business challenges faced by high potential and emerging professional women leaders. Jane has coached women in the Executive Leadership Program and has extensive experience mentoring scientists, senior leaders and middle managers.

Her degrees and certifications include an MSS in group dynamics from Bryn Mawr College, a BA in International Relations from the University of Pennsylvania, and certifications to administer Achieve Global's Leadership for Results, DiSC, SCOPE, a stress management training program, Myers-Briggs and FIRO-B. Jane serves on the boards of the Association for Quality and Participation and the National Defense Industrial Association. She is also a Mentor for Women Unlimited Leadership program candidates.

Her community involvement includes serving on the Board of Girls Inc., being a reviewer for the Women's Way Community Fund, and serving on the Advisory Committee for Career Wardrobe.

Jane Lowenstein
Philadelphia, PA
215.482.1577
jlowenstein@janbara.com
www.JanBara.com

Barbara Taylor
Philadelphia, PA
215.481.9588
btaylor@janbara.com
www.JanBara.com

Barbara Taylor & Jane Lowenstein

Chapter 6

Jim Kouzes

David E. Wright (Wright)

Today we are talking to Jim Kouzes, a popular seminar and conference speaker. He shares his insights about the leadership practices that contribute to high performance in individuals and organizations. He leaves his audiences with practical leadership tools and tips that they can apply at work, at home, and in their communities. Jim is Chairman Americus of the Tom Peters Company, a professional services firm that specializes in leadership development. He is also an executive fellow in the Center for Innovation and Entrepreneurship, Leavey School of Business, Santa Clara University. Jim is the co-author of the award winning book, *The Leadership Challenge*, which is now in its third edition with over one million copies sold. *The Leadership Challenge*, available in eleven languages was a selection of the McMillan Executive Book Club and the Fortune Book Club. It's the winner of the James A. Hamilton Hospital Administrators' Book Award and Critics Choice Award. Jim also co-authored *Credibility: How Leaders Gain and Lose It: Why People Demand it,* which was chosen by Industry Week as one of the ten best management books of the year as well as *Encouraging The Heart, The Leadership Journal, The Leadership Challenge Workbook*, and *The Leadership Practices Inventory*. Mr. Kouzes, welcome to *Leading the Way to Success*!

Jim Kouzes (Kouzes)

Thank you, David. It's a pleasure to be here.

Wright

Jim, today we're talking about success. In 2001, the International Management Council honored you with the prestigious Wilbur M. McFeely award. Past recipients include Peter Drucker, Lee Iacocca, Tom Peters, Ken Blanchard, Norman Vincent Peale, and Stephen Covey. Some would argue that this kind of recognition by ones peers denotes success more than money or position. What do you think?

Kouzes

David, the award, the McFeely Award, was a recognition that went to both Barry Posner and myself for our body of work. This began with *Leadership Challenge* and has continued in a collaboration that's lasted 20 years. That's far longer than many marriages. Any success that I may have achieved is a result of being blessed with a wonderful family, generous and supportive friends, and a great deal of luck. I can't claim self-credit for my accomplishments. You know I had the honor of interviewing Don Bennett who was the first amputee ever to climb Mt. Rainier, that's 14,410 feet, on one leg and two crutches. I asked him to tell me what the most important lesson was that he learned on that historic climb. He replied, "You can't do it alone." That message has always stuck with me. Not a day goes by when I don't think about that. It also keeps me humble and grateful. It's indeed an honor to be included with that esteemed company. Knowing that others appreciate our work and believe we've made a contribution to the field is affirming and very sustaining. It helps me get up in the morning.

Wright

I can imagine!

Kouzes

Yeah, it will last a lifetime. Money and position or momentary fame are very fleeting in its emerald. The real gift is the gift that others give to you of their own recognition for your contribution. I am very grateful. You're absolutely right in that recognition of peers is more important than anything.

Wright

You are acknowledged as an expert on leadership. Do you have a working definition of success that you apply to yourself and to others?

Kouzes

I have learned so much from the leaders that I've interviewed. This question reminds me of an interview I had with Major General John Stanford. He had set up the Military Traffic Command for the U.S. Army and then went on to be County Administrator, Fulton County, Georgia, and then on to become Superintendent of Schools in Seattle School District before he passed away. I asked him the question of how do you develop leaders for the future. He answered, "When anyone asks me that question, I tell them I have the secret to success in life." Your question reminded me of John's response. He said, "The secret to success is: Stay in love. Staying in love gives you the fire to really ignite other people, to see inside other people, to get more things done than other people. A person who is not in love doesn't really feel the kind of excitement that helps him to get ahead and to lead others to achieve. I don't know any other tire or anything in life that is more exhilarating and powerful a feeling than love is." Now, Wow! Huh? So I can tell you I didn't expect to hear that from the Major General of the United States Army. But, in thinking about all the people that we've interviewed, John among them and many others, that response makes complete sense to me. Success is defined by how I feel, not what I possess.

Wright

Will you tell our readers a little bit about how you got started in business, and why you continue to do what you do?

Kouzes

I think it was the summer of 1969, David. I had just returned to the U.S. from Turkey where I had served in the Peace Corps for two years. I was 24 years old, and I was looking for a job. I still wanted to make a difference in the world. When I came back I was fortunate enough to be able to find a job in Austin, Texas, where I had fallen in love with Donna Burns who later became my wife for 30 years until her passing in 2000. I found a job working for Community Action Program Training Institute where we travel around and do trainings for people in management, leadership, communications, and interpersonal skills, who had been working in the war on poverty effort. That led me to become involved with people from various organizations involved in the applied behavioral sciences, the people who did tea groups and sensitivity training and cross cultural training, which then lead to work at University of Texas, San Jose State University, and then finally Santa Clara University where I ended up meeting Barry. So while the path took me in some respects around the world and to various states in the U.S., there was one clear common theme throughout everything which was training and development to help people learn better how to manage, lead, and work with others in teams. So my collaboration with Barry was really a continuation of that, but it's been the most productive period of my life since getting together with him.

Wright

Your client list reads like a "Who's Who" in business and industry: AT&T, Bowing, Charles Schwab, Federal Express, and Dell Computer just to name a few of them. Your success must drive their motivation to use their services. What do you think organizations look for as they contact experts to help them?

Kouzes

David, in our research we found that credibility is the foundation of leadership. What my clients and my colleagues' clients look for is very akin to the same thing they look for in leaders, which is personal credibility. David, I think they are asking themselves, "Does he know what he's talking about? Does he have the expertise? Does he have the evidence to support it? Does he have the relevant experience? Can I trust him with the health and success of my business? Does he have my business interests at heart or is he in it for himself? Does he show up on time? Does he deliver what he promises? Does he say no when he can't deliver? Does he have the energy to see us through there?" They are asking themselves all those questions, but what that adds up to in one word is credibility. I really firmly believe, David, that what all professionals have to offer their clients is very simply their personal credibility, the most important personal asset I have, and I'll protect it with every fiber in my being.

Wright

The Wall Street Journal has cited you as one of the twelve most requested non-university executive education providers to United States companies. Could this be one of the keys to your success, the ability to take the message directly to the people who need it in a place convenient to them?

Kouzes

Very early on in my career, David, I was blessed with the opportunity to work with some of the most seasoned professionals in the business. One of the things I learned early on from a guy named Fred Margolis, who was a master trainer, was how learning takes place. I remember having lunch with Fred at an Italian Restaurant in Washington, D.C. He said to me, "Jim, what's the best way to learn something?" I always remember this scene. I thought I knew the answer because I'd been to a lot of experiential training. I said, "Well, the best way to learn something is to experience it yourself." I was very convinced that that was the right answer. He said, "No, the best way to learn something is to teach it to somebody else." I said, "Wow!" You know there are moments when you are asked to give a speech, David, or you're asked to teach your kids, or you're asked to lead a team of people and help acquaint them with a new software program or with a new procedure. Those are times when you know you really have to prepare yourself. You have to think, how am I going to transfer what I learned to somebody else? We all have experienced that, and Fred was very astute in saying, "Yes, it's about experience. We all have to go through it ourselves. But when you also are going to have to transfer that lesson to somebody else, that's when you really learn the best. We learn the best when we teach someone else." What I've tried to do is shape my style of training and development and of speaking. Even when I give a lecture, I'll always engage the audience, and I always ask them questions because I know that from their experience they have the answers. That is in fact how we did our research. We asked people to tell us their stories. So the richness in this lesson of we learn best when we teach someone else has influenced everything I do. I think the best teachers and learners are master storytellers. That's very much what I think people want. Every time I give a talk, people say, "Well, give me an example of this. Give me an example of that. How does this apply in my situation?" So, while people want data, they want the evidence that what you are saying works, because in business you want evidence. You want something that works. They also want to know the stories and the examples.

Wright

Well, I've never thought of it that way before. I've always thought right off the top of my head that experiential learning would be the greatest of all learning models, but as I reflect on my life, you are absolutely true, or what he said was absolutely true.

Kouzes

Well, thank you. As you see it's very interesting. It was one of the epiphanious moments.

Wright

I'm fascinated by the amount of research you did in your book, *Leadership Challenge*. While talking to leaders all over the United States, did you get a sense that leaders are successful, or is leadership and success two entirely different subjects?

Kouzes

Originally my colleague and co-author, Barry Posner, along with Willis Brown corroborated on a research project done both in the U.S. and Canada. They looked at learning and leading. They found that those executives, who were more actively engaged in learning, are rated by others as more effective leaders. So there's a positive correlation to learning and leading. The other important thing about that study is that they also found that it didn't matter what your learning style was. What mattered is that you use more of whatever your style was. In response to your question, I think that the message is very clear. You keep on learning throughout your life if you want to succeed. It's the learning that really comes first, and then everything else will follow.

Wright

Without using CEOs, well-known leaders or people of wealth, could you help our readers understand how the average Joe Homemaker, the student, attains success as they discharge their commitments and live their lives that are not in the spotlight?

Kouzes

Well, David, one of the things Barry and I decided early on was not to study CEOs. I know a whole bunch of them, and I have a great deal of respect for them. But we felt early on that it was important to study people in the middle and on the front lines. There is this myth in our society that success and power and importance is associated with position. If you are on the top, you're a success. So, everybody strives to be Chief Executive Officer. Everybody strives to be on the cover of Fortune Magazine. Everybody strives to be the number one guy or gal in the organization. You know, it's just been us! I don't think that success and being on top, being in the spotlight, is really one in the same thing. I have been known to look straight in the eyes of a Chief Executive Officer sitting in the audience and say, "With all due respect, you are not the most important person in this room." The audience often gasps at that, you know, "God, this guy just insulted my Chief Executive Officer!" Of course, I've told them ahead of time or her ahead of time, that I'm going to do this because we need to make this point. And normally the CEO will nod and agree with me. Then I will say, "The most important person in this room right now is each and every one of you. And to the members of your team you are the most important leader in this organization. It's you, not the Chief Executive Officer, who has the most impact on your day today performance." And, David, it is absolutely true that the research clearly indicates that the most important person in any relationship is that most immediate supervisor, if it's an organization. So, if it's in a family, whomever it might be, your mother or your father. If it's on a project team, it's the team leader. We, each and every one of us, can make a difference because we have an impact on those closest to us. So there is really no difference in the behavior between a Chief Executive Officer and a front line employee, or even a parent when it comes to leadership. It's all the same behavior.

Wright

Jim, as a Boy Scout, you were chosen to participate in the inauguration of John F. Kennedy. Later you worked two years in the Peace Corps.

Jim Kouzes

Somewhere in the definition of success must be a charge to give back to the community or to the world some of what you have received. Is that true? If so, how do you suggest worthwhile projects to others?

Kouzes

I think, David, you are right. There comes a time in our lives, and it's often in the later years of our lives, halftime as Bob Buford has noted, when we feel the need to go from success to significance, when we move from thinking about material things to wanting to leave a legacy and make a contribution. I was very fortunate and very blessed to grow up in a family where early on in my life my mother was very active in the United Nations Association in our church. So was my father. He was a civil servant and he took that role very seriously. When I joined the Peace Corps, I was involved in social services for 12 years. I think there is nothing more honorable, in my opinion, than serving others. Max Dupree, the former Chief Executive Officer of Harmon Miller once said that the first job as a leader was to define reality. The last was to say thank you. In between, it was to be a servant and a debtor. I found this to be a very profound statement and one that can only come from someone with a caring heart. God has given us a chance in this life to receive or to give. I learned early on that it is better to give than to receive. But you know what? When you give, you also get more back in your life so many times fold what you give. I think the kinds of projects I would recommend that people engage in are those that come from their hearts. Whether its your community, the environment, church, some political change you want to make that has to do with social justice, serving the poor and the needy, doing something for your kids, or your school or whatever is in your heart. At the end of the day, you'll sleep a lot better knowing that you have provided a service to someone else.

Wright

You know success is so allusive for some. I've known many people who have had great ideas, but just never seemed to get things going. Is there a formula that will make success more reachable, or is most success simply a function of being in the right place at the right time?

Kouzes

I'd say I'd feel might lucky in my life and I could never have planned my life the way it's turned out. I think that the whole notion of career planning is that to me it is a foreign concept. I couldn't have planned to run into Barry Posner, and then find out that we had a common interest, and planned to write half a dozen or actually 10 books together now, you know. I mean, that wasn't in the plan anywhere. It was serendipity which by way is from a book by Horrace Walpole entitled and reprinted as *Serendip*. It was simply by combination of sarcasity and love that we were able to succeed. I think the common thread in my life and in the life of others who have been so fortunate is that I followed my calling. Luck comes to those who follow their calling. Success comes to those who follow their heart. Yet when I was giving a talk to a group of educators in university level, college level educators, a few weeks ago, and I asked them, "How many of you have been involved in career planning with your students?" and a lot of them raised their hands. Then I said, "Well, how many of you have talked to them about their calling?" Nobody raised his hand. So we engage in this conversation with young people and with ourselves about how we can plan our careers but we never really think deeply about our true calling. A theologian and novelist once commented, I'm paraphrasing here, but I think he said something to the effect that you find your great call where your great joy meets the world's great need. I think that comes as close to a formula for success as I can find. Watch your great joy. Watch the great need in the world that enables you to use your great joy and therein lies your calling.

Wright

What are some of the projects that you have planned for yourself for the future to insure you happiness and success?

Kouzes

Well, I'm just finishing up I think it's our 10th book together. This one is an edited volume that is written. It's called *Christian Collections on Leadership Challenge*. We had five other colleagues who are Christian leaders reflect on each of our five practices, and we wrote the beginning and the closing to that. We are doing more work now with secondary schools and there'll probably be another book project come out of educational leadership. Of course, I'm continuing to do my own work in speaking with clients and doing consulting and training around leadership. One thing I have to say, David, is that leadership is my calling, and I'm going to stick with that for the remainder of my career. I'm not going to try to change jobs or change my profession. That I have I'll stay with. But I have picked up golf. I learned golf late in life after my wife passed away. It's a wonderfully humbling game. It also helps me to engage in a personal challenge and see if I can still learn to do anything new. But those are some of the projects I've got planned for myself. Barry and I are also sitting down and outlining a new book, which will be related more to leadership as personal, some of the personal sides of leadership that we've learned over the years that are so important.

Wright

I've got a theory after playing for many, many years that if you could find a hundred people who had scarred wrists from trying to slice them, 98 of them would be golfers. It is a humbling game, isn't it?

Kouzes

Yeah, well after watching the British Open and seeing some of the best golfers in the world end up with scores over par because the course was so difficult, then a guy who's never won a major before or any tournament before competing in his first major win it, it's a pretty amazing feat. In that is there is hope for all of us.

Wright

That's right.

Kouzes

It's also a great lesson in that just because you are one of the best golfers in the world doesn't mean you'll win every weekend. You know one of the things I love about learning this game is that it is a personal challenge. I was never one who was fond of sports metaphors. It just seemed to me that if you weren't active, you probably couldn't relate. But now that I've engaged in this, I'm finding all kinds of relevance to it. It's a wonderful game that for me is helping me to stay active and also learn something new. But that's my leisure and pleasure activity thing now.

Wright

Do you have any thoughts that might lead our readers to discover ways in which they might reach for more success in their businesses as well as their personal lives?

Kouzes

I'm of the belief that we actually don't reach for success. Success is not a thing out there that you can actually grab onto. It's not really a destination. It's a path that you travel down. You'll know you're on the right path if you keep finding joy along the way. If you keep leading people you can really call your friends, if you keep hearing your inner voice urging you to continue forward, if you find yourself constantly in awe and in wonder at all the opportunities for learning and growth. I think if you get all those messages daily, then you're on the path to success and your destination may never arrive, but you'll always know that you're on the right path.

Wright

Very interesting. Well, what an interesting conversation on leadership, Jim, and I really appreciate the time you have taken with me today. I know how busy your schedule is, and I really appreciate you taking this time.

Kouzes

It's always a lot of fun, David. Thank you very much. I appreciate it and stay in love.

Wright

I will. Today we have been talking to Jim Kouzes, who is a popular author and seminar and conference speaker. He teaches people how to increase their individual performance as well as we have found out today a lot of other things. Thank you so much, Jim, for being with us.

Kouzes

It's my pleasure, David, thank you for the opportunity.

About the Author

Jim Kouzes is the coauthor with Barry Posner of the award-winning and best-selling book, *The Leadership Challenge,* with over 1.5 million copies sold. He's also the Dean's Executive Professor of Leadership, Leavey School of Business, Santa Clara University.

Jim and Barry developed the widely used and highly acclaimed *Leadership Practices Inventory* (LPI), a 360° questionnaire assessing leadership behavior. The LPI has been administered to over 500,000 leaders, and over 3 million observers worldwide have provided feedback using the LPI. It is the top-selling off-the-shelf leadership assessment instrument in the world. Over 350 doctoral dissertations and academic research projects have been based on their work.

Jim is also an experienced executive. He served as president, then CEO and chairman of the Tom Peters Company from 1988-until 2000. Prior to his tenure at TPC he directed the Executive Development Center at Santa Clara University from 1981 through 1987. He also founded the Joint Center for Human Services Development at San Jose State University, which he directed from 1972 until 1980. Jim's commitment to service was nurtured during his years growing up in the Washington, D.C. area. His lifelong career in education began in 1967-1969 when he served for two years in the Peace Corps. Jim believes it was on January 20, 1961 when he was first inspired to dedicate himself to leadership. That was the day he was one of only a dozen Eagle **Kouzes Bio**

Scouts who served in John F. Kennedy's Honor Guard at the Presidential Inauguration. Jim can be reached at jim@kouzes.com, or on the Web at www.leadershipchallenge.com.

Chapter 7

Rozhy Talisman

David Wright (Wright)

Today we're talking with Rozhy Talisman. Get ready for an uplifting, inspirational journey with Rozhy Talisman, the universal motivator. She will transport you to the world of creating your happiness and make your dreams come true. Rozhy is author of the book, *The Art of Creating Your Happiness.*

She says to everyone, "My best university has been life. It is an art to learn to be happy and this is not taught at universities; we need to be happy to gain success."

"Your smile is your talisman, you recharge us with your energy," said her record producer.

Read her books, witness her in person, smile, and sing along; it will be an experience of a lifetime.

Rozhy, welcome to *Leading the Way to Success!*

Rozhy Talisman (Talisman)

Thank you very much David. I am very, very glad and honored to be here, to be part of all of you.

Wright

So *The Art of Creating Your Happiness* is an interesting title for your book; how did you choose it?

Talisman

I wanted to incite curiosity in my readers because who does not want to be happy? The response I've had so far is great. I am deeply honored to be a vehicle to bring my concept of true happiness to everyone who wishes to pursue it.

The journey to happiness is not easy, though it is enjoyable. With enthusiasm, discipline, and perseverance it is fully accessible to everyone. If I have been able to do it, you all, my dear readers, will also conquer the precious art of true happiness, sooner than you even imagine.

Happiness can be defined in many different ways. To me, happiness leads the way to success, and I choose to live by the kind of success that is based on internal happiness. This inner skill gives you the foundation for all the branches of success. Being truly happy also grants you the patience and knowledge needed to pursue emotional growth and financial achievements.

I remember when I was about seven years old, my parents' friends used to comment, "What a nice mood your little girl has. She speaks with her eyes." I also remember my teachers saying to my parents, "Your daughter is a happy girl; her eyes have a special spark; she transmits happiness." At that time I had no idea what they were talking about and I did not know what to say. Only one thing I knew for sure, that my parents were very proud of me. This feeling led me to start my quest of better understanding happiness, its origin, and the different ways of discovering and living it. Part of this journey is helping others find it too.

I later realized all these people had a very important purpose in my life. They taught me that happiness comes from inside because they saw it through my eyes and attitude, they all contributed to making me feel special. You are special too; everyone has a dormant artist within and the potential to awaken it to reach true happiness.

The "University of My Life" has now given me the keys to a formula for happiness—the principles and values I fully share in my book, *The Art of Creating Your Happiness.*

Wright

What is happiness to you?

Talisman

Happiness to me is the reason for being alive. I cannot imagine life without joy and bliss. Achieving true happiness brings a healthier and more fulfilled life. I have tried for many years to find a simple yet all-encompassing definition for permanent happiness. This is what I have found: "True happiness is the awakening to the fantastic journey of one's consciousness; it is the awareness of one's inner potential as children of a Higher Being."

Simple things that are true happiness to me are, for example: looking at a baby, smelling a flower, observing a multicolored butterfly, hearing music or the birds singing or the wind whispering, watching the infinite ocean and the seagulls dance around the mischievous waves, looking at the ethereal clouds fly along with the wind, feeling the sensation of every breath I take and every beat of my heart, laughing with my beloved ones, writing and speaking about the art of creating your happiness, and much more.

Being truly happy is also knowing how to slow down during one's daily activities, observing and appreciating the little but big details we tend to overlook. It is also reminding ourselves to value and cherish the present moment because "the now" is all we have—it's our reality and gift. The past is gone and the future does not exist yet.

When I discovered the connection with my Higher Self, I understood the difference between temporary versus long-lasting happiness. I learned that material possessions, power, money, and artificial beauty are fun and provide pleasure but not permanent happiness. Happiness is always within you. I also learned that by applying inner focus and strength, soon you discover the treasures contained in the interior of your being.

Wright

So why do you say that happiness is an art?

Talisman

First If I may, I would like to give you my definition of both happiness and art and how they blend and harmonize perfectly as a magical melody.

Art is a skill that can be acquired. It expresses culture, beauty, and refinement. Happiness is a dormant virtue everyone possesses. It can be awakened and mastered by every one of us. There are many kinds of art.

For example, cooking, walking, speaking, performing, painting, smiling, playing music, selling—these are just a few to mention.

Every human being is a natural artist of some kind. The way to discover the artist within is by immersing yourself in the interior of your being or true inner self and be willing to awaken your sleepy artist. You will be amazed at the treasures you will discover—even if you have thought in the past that you were not an artist, I believe you *are* an artist.

Happiness is the foundation of all arts and virtues. There are several steps to educate yourself in this art. A good start is to read my book *The Art of Creating your Happiness*. In the book I reveal a formula with seven magical principles that will provide you with the necessary tools to reach happiness and success. I also include some activities and exercises to feel energized and spiritually nurtured. To be able to learn this art, all you need is enthusiasm, determination, and practice. Remember: practice makes perfect.

Being truly happy is not a privilege that only a few people are chosen to enjoy. In the same way one can learn any other form of art, happiness can be learned and achieved by you, me, and the rest of the world.

Naturally, as we all know, the environment we grew up in determines most of our personality, habits, and limitations. Nevertheless, today, as adults, considering the free will we were granted with, we have the option to make changes, be happier, and lead a more harmonious life. Your gifts are hidden inside of you. Go ahead—venture within you, discover them, and very soon you will reach the most distant stars.

Wright

How do people discover their inner gift?

Talisman

To discover one's inner gift, I recommend that you first of all learn to be still and quiet then go inward and connect with your true self, who lives in the center of your being, and listen very carefully. Feel the sensations and the way it feels when you finally make the connection. Listen very carefully, maybe at the beginning you will not understand its language; the quieter you become though, the easier it will be for you to be aware of your inner gifts.

For this to happen, I recommend the following exercise: find a quiet place with a relaxing atmosphere and practice your voyage to the inside of your being. You must be comfortable and as silent as possible. Sit or lie down, take ten or fifteen deep breaths until your mind becomes relaxed, and still. Practice this process until your mind does not generate thoughts. This state is called meditative.

When you reach the desired meditative state, you are now connecting with your inner self. You have left the present dimension and you have started to become one with your true self—the one who is connected with the Higher Self. You may call your Higher Self God, Superior Being, Creator, etc., depending on your religious beliefs. At this point you feel as one with the Whole and the Universe—you have fused with your inner being. It is a beautiful experience.

To complement your wonderful discovery, I also encourage you to educate yourself and engage in uplifting activities. I highly recommend that you watch and read only inspirational movies and books. The conversations and the people you surround yourself with are very important too. The process of discovering your natural artist happens very fast, it's like abruptly waking up from a deep sleep or the feeling of not being able to breathe while swimming under the water, and rushing up to the surface to finally take a deep breath of oxygen; imagine this wonderful sensation of your lungs expanding at their fullest capacity!

This whole process is a renewal of your being—it feels as though a new you has just been born. People will start asking you questions such as, "You look younger, what are you doing? You look different, what's up with you?" Of course, they will ask these questions because people will notice you are different—maybe more peaceful and confident. You now express your hidden treasures and artistic inner gifts. You have discovered with certainty that you are not alone. None of us is alone.

Wright

What do you mean when you say you can create your own happiness?

Talisman

Based on the Natural Law of Energy, everything that moves the material world is based on energy. All forms of life are energy in motion manifested in matter. One of the major rules of this Law of Energy that I would like you to remember is this: "Our thoughts and feelings are energy," and since energy always needs matter to manifest, be aware of the kinds of thoughts your mind generates because they create your reality. We are the creators of our own destiny. This is what I mean when I say you can create your own happiness—we create our world with our thoughts, feelings, words, and actions.

The recognition of our essence as co-creators is closely linked to the discovery of the connection between one's true self and one's Higher Self, as well as the relation between the world of energy and matter. I elaborate deeper into these concepts in my book.

The acceptance of this powerful truth brings us a great responsibility. When you refer yourself to creating your destiny and acknowledging your energy potentials, remember to think, feel, act, and speak with humility. Always keep your ego under control. Notice I will mention several times the importance of keeping one's ego under control. What I mean by saying "keep your ego under control" is disciplining one's mind by developing wisdom. The development of wisdom involves learning to recognize and differentiate our two inner voices: the voice of the ego and the voice of the soul.

The voice of your ego is always making you believe you are special and advises you to demand the attention over others—it tells you to compete and win no matter what you have to do; it tells you to criticize others and/or put them down; it incites you to get easily insulted and bothered, etc.

On the other hand, your inner voice of the soul always advises in such a way that leaves you with peaceful and honorable feelings.

The Law of Attraction is a derivative of the Natural Law of Energy, and since energy is in constant motion and will eventually manifest, one must be aware of the importance of generating and producing only constructive thoughts and feelings because they will materialize sooner or later, thus determining your reality. The Law of Attraction attracts what you talk about and focus on. Focus on the positive and that is what the law of attraction will grant you. "Talk about what you don't want and you will have what you don't want present in your life," this is a powerful concept expressed by the author, Dr. Wayne Dyer, in his book *The Power of Intention*.

In conclusion, to create happiness it's necessary to recognize your potential as co-creator and always remember to be humble and act accordingly. It is a big responsibility you have undertaken. Listen to the voice of your soul, be aware of your thoughts and feelings, and focus on the positive of what you want to have in your life.

Wright

Have you always been a happy person?

Talisman

Yes, I have always been a happy person. Don't misunderstand me—this does not mean I don't know suffering and pain. It just means I learned to decipher the enigma that lies behind harsh experiences. It is necessary to look at the positive side and find the solution. Always try to find the lesson behind each painful situation and soon you will empower yourself by assimilating the value these lessons signify.

I grew up in Mexico and in my early childhood I lived with my grandmother, Mama Mia. I remember how happy I was, even though we were poor. Of course when one is three or four years old, the concept of poor or rich does not exist, those labels are learned later in life.

Mama Mia taught me beautiful virtues and one of them was to appreciate and value what we had. I don't remember ever wishing to have something I didn't have. I learned to cook, sweep, mop, and water the flowers. I enjoyed a simple life and authentic people. I even helped her sell rice, sugar, and beans in a little convenience store she owned.

I always had to finish my food—she never let me leave any food on my plate. She used to tell me, "Serve yourself only what you will eat; there are other kids in the world who are not as lucky as you are, and they're starving; they don't have enough food."

I have learned valuable principles since then, and now as an adult, I still remember these lessons; I realize how lucky I am. I don't need material possessions to be happy. I enjoy them, but I realize we are not who we are because of what our title is or what we own. We are beyond material, we are eternal beings, and it's about time that we start taking responsibilities and living accordingly. It is necessary to feel the lack of things to be able to appreciate and value what has been given. It is necessary to feel pain to appreciate happiness. It is necessary to fall down and be able to stand up without shame or self-pity, and it is necessary to go through darkness to see the light again.

The experiences learned throughout our life are precious lessons and are part of who we are today.

Having said this, I ask you to close the painful chapters, leave them where they belong—in the past. Simply take from those experiences the lessons learned and continue your journey focusing on the now. Cherish and value the present moment; it is time to open yourself to the land of infinite probabilities or "the infinite field of possibilities." These are the words of author Dr. Deepak Chopra from his book *The Seven Spiritual Laws to Success*.

Instead, observe the beauty and the treasures life offers you every minute. This is your reality. Do you see how fortunate you are?

Wright

I'm not happy all the time, but I am content this way, so why should I learn your formula?

Talisman

You might think you are content, and in reality you may not be unhappy, but you may also be far from being truly happy. This is a little bit like a puzzle, but I'll explain.

Everyone has experienced fairly happy moments and fun moments temporarily. However, after the excitement and pleasure are gone, reality hits us, and again we feel boredom and emptiness. These moments and circumstances of course are not what true happiness is.

If you feel fine but not great, I have my doubts about the kind of happiness you experience.

If you are open to the infinite land of possibilities, then why not venture out and learn my magic formula? There is a way for you to know if it is indeed true happiness that you are experiencing or if your ego is advising you to avoid disciplining your mind. It is common for the mind to play tricks. This is what I would recommend, it is a little test: ask some of your loved ones the following questions:

1. Do I make you happy?
2. Do you think I'm pleasant to be around?
3. Am I a role model to you?
4. Do I contribute in any way to your happiness?
5. Do you think I am a happy—*truly* happy—person?

These questions should be enough for you to find out the truth. Do not get upset at the answers you hear. Be receptive and open-minded. The objective is for you to know if you see yourself in the same way that people who care about you perceive you.

The only way to self-improvement is to recognize and accept one's defects and weaknesses. The first time I did this I was in shock. I was not nearly the person I thought I was. It was hard for me to accept the truth but I had to because the opinion of my family and dear friends was the most honest. People who love us are our best and toughest judges. Good luck in your findings.

As soon as you find out the truth and you are willing to make the needed changes in your life, I recommend you take the following steps: First recognize and accept your wrongs and second, correct them. It is not difficult—if you are determined to do it. Time passes fast and when the glamour of your life slows down and autumn knocks on your door, at this stage you will pick up what was planted in your spring. Before that day comes, ask yourself, "What kinds of seeds am I planting?"

Happiness is what one should pick up—the everlasting virtue that originates inside of our being and is fun and exciting—it does not change with the years, it does not have a price, and will be part of us wherever we go.

Wright

Why focus on one's happiness when there is so much misery and poverty in the world?

Talisman

That's a great question. This is precisely the time to focus on our happiness. By being happy we can help others reach happiness too. By building wealth we can also offer our physical or financial support to those in need. Keep in mind that the foundation of the Law of Attraction consists of focusing on what you want and this is what the energetic cosmos will give back to you. Yes, we should be compassionate, but we should not focus on misery and poverty because we will attract that into our lives. Instead, we must create wealth and happiness in order to spread our wings and make a difference in people's lives.

Working together we can impact the world by creating a collective consciousness to uplift the spirit of mankind. The more we share our knowledge with others and contribute to the betterment of humanity, the more doors will open to achieve our goals and dreams. No matter what the circumstances are, there is always a choice we can make. We can go through difficult situations involving pain and suffering and we still have the choice to face adversity with a positive or a negative attitude.

A positive attitude consists of learning from our experiences and extracting the good. This is the only way for us to endure and be able to also help others strengthen their spirits. Keep in mind that there is a reason for everything that happens.

On the other hand, a negative attitude would be to blame others for our suffering, complaining, or feeling sorry for ourselves and others. We cannot help others with this attitude—we make them weaker and will only encourage them to get depressed and confused.

In the same way, the rivers naturally flow into the ocean pushing debris out to the shore and our mother earth absorbs the excess of a heavy storm and the sun evaporates the stagnant waters. And in the same manner, the trees sleep throughout a snowy winter season and in spring they turn green again. Exactly in the same way, when we focus on the positive side of situations and stop worrying about the results, the solution appears with surprising, beautiful answers and everything gets resolved naturally.

Yes, we all have the choice to think, feel, and act positively instead of negatively to attract happiness and help others reach happiness too. By doing so, in time, everything in your life will fall into place and you by yourself made it happen.

Relinquish your desire to be in control and believe without doubts or questions that everything will be okay and according to your wishes. I explain more in depth the importance of focusing on the positive and believing with blind faith in my book *The Art of Creating Your Happiness.*

Wright

How about people who lose loved ones and experience tragedies? How can they be happy?

Talisman

It is not easy. Let's go back to the basic function of the universal natural laws of energy for a minute. Energy is in constant motion and its physical manifestation is based in the life cycle. Everything happens for a reason, and as human beings we are not here by accident. We have a purpose to accomplish and so does the rest of Nature—every living form has a function to perform.

Besides Nature's purpose or function, there is also a beginning and an end for all physical life forms. That is why in my book, *The Art of Creating Your Happiness*, I describe the importance of mankind returning to its essence or origin. When mankind reunites with Nature and learns to go inward to connect with the Higher Self, it will be easier to understand how nature's lifecycle works. As a result, the mystery of life and death will have a different meaning and one will understand that we *all* have a purpose to get here and to depart.

Those who better understand nature and the cosmic and divine laws should take responsibility to transmit this awareness to the ones who have lost family and friends and are in need of compassion and consolation. Their pain is worsened when the losses are traumatic and tragic. It's very important to help others understand their dear ones who passed away under these circumstances by recognizing, acknowledging and elevating their purpose.

I came to the realization that the ones who make me suffer the most throughout my life also contributed greatly to the person I am today. In cases when someone who has made others and their families suffer passes, this person should be thanked and appreciated.

I remember my first husband and the tears I shed because of his infidelity. A few years before he died I thanked him for making me grow strong and view life from a different perspective. There are always reasons to pay attention and honor the message and treasures they leave us. Many times we learn more after they leave than during the whole time they were with us on this earth. We need to let our departed ones know that we are okay, happy, and in peace. This enables them to be able to rest in peace and continue their journey.

The spark of life is pure energy and resides inside of our physical being. It is the connection with our Divine Source that keeps our heart beating and our body kicking. Remember again that we are spiritual beings learning to live inside of a physical body and we are part of nature. Every form of life that exists on this planet has a purpose with a beginning and an end. Mankind is part of Nature and so is the whole cosmos. Energy is in constant motion of renewal and so are we. Nature is energy; energy is everlasting and indestructible, and it never changes. We are all connected.

Wright

So why do you call your formula "magical"?

Talisman

It is magical because you learn to do miracles. When I discovered this formula and started applying and practicing the seven principles contained in it, I consciously started creating and manifesting my dreams. As a matter of fact, I remember my dreams started to become reality since I was a child, however, I did not realize at that time why this was happening.

One day when I was twenty-two years old, I decided to pay attention to what I was doing to make my dreams come true, and so I did. This was the beginning of the discovery of my Magic Formula. Then I got very busy raising five children, and as time passed by I read many books. Some of them impacted my life and motivated me to transmit my magic formula to those who wanted to learn and practice it. So I wrote my first book *The Art of Creating Your Happiness* in 2008. I was offered the opportunity to co-author with Jack Canfield *Leading the Way to Success*—the chapter you are reading now.

Among the authors who inspired my writing were George Adamski, Linda Goodman, Deepak Chopra, Rosario Morales, Wayne Dyer, Jack Canfield, and most recently all, the spiritual teachers and philosophers who participated in the movie *The Secret*. If they could do it, I can do it, and if I can do it, you can do it. Soon you will do magic too. That is why I say that my formula and its principles are "magical"—because it gives you the way to create the life of your dreams.

The seven principles are numbered in the order recommended to be learned and applied. Being consistent is necessary to achieve maximum results. These precious principles give you the tools and the key to open the door to happiness and success.

In my book I also guide you to a better understanding of how the laws of energy work and how they are intimately related to us and our destiny. You will learn to transform your thoughts and feelings and apply techniques to convert the negative into positive. Your mind will learn to organize its wishes and desires in such a way that soon you will know exactly how you would like them to be manifested. This means you will fully comprehend the process to pursue your dreams and turn them into reality. I call this magic, don't you?

The closer you get to what you pursue, the wiser you become. Your natural artist will soon emerge ready to explore, enjoy, and create the life you have always dreamed of having. You will perfect your skills as a co-creator (remember to always keep a humble attitude). Soon you will start making more honorable decisions because you now understand that you are creating the life you want. Get ready to grab the steering wheel and take control of your life. And most importantly, help others achieve happiness too.

And now, be ready to become the creator of your happiness and lead the way to success.

Wright

Would you give our readers a brief explanation of what the seven magical principles are?

Talisman

Sure, I am describing them briefly for you in this chapter. I go into greater detail about their meaning and functions in my book. These are the seven principles, and they are mentioned in the order I recommend that they be learned and practiced:

Give. Give thanks—give physically, emotionally, or spiritually from yourself; give love—love always.

Ask. Ask specifically what you wish to receive—ask with modesty and in an organized manner.

Visualize. Visualization is the beginning of creating—it combines thinking and imagining.

Believe. Believe with certainty what you visualize—believe in yourself and believe in your dreams.

Smile. Smile always—give the treasure of your smile to others. Having a nice attitude moves the whole world.

Receive. Receive gracefully and with appreciation. Receive and share.

Thank. Be thankful—always be thankful for what you are, represent, and possess. Be always appreciative; say thank you.

Notice how the principles number one and number seven (first and last) contain the secret code of this formula because both mention giving thanks. Being thankful is vital for this formula to succeed. We should always be thankful and cherish what we have. Before, during, and after one's daily activities, remember to say thank you.

To remind myself about thanking, I carry a necklace as a talisman. Each time I touch it I sing the song, "Thank You, Thank You." I composed this song "Thank You" to give to all of you. When you get the book, ask for the CD with the same name, *The Art of Creating your Happiness.* I hope you enjoy it.

When you learn this magic formula, embrace it; engrave it in your heart. It is part of you—it is now yours too.

You already know what the seven magical principles are; I hope you enjoy learning and practicing them. In my book you will also find a mini-dictionary to help you better understand the meaning and application of each key word.

I assure you that the journey you are about to embark on will be unique and exciting. Go confidently in the direction of your dreams and you will soon start reaping the fruits of the seeds you will be planting along your path.

Oh, and please don't forget to help others too.

Wright

So how long does it take to see the results?

Talisman

Great question. How long will it take is based on how long will it take for you to read the book, learn the formula and the seven principles, apply them, and practice them. I guess it will depend on each person. I recommend that you first fully understand the main rule of the Law of Energy based on the principle that teaches us to be always *aware* of the thoughts and feelings we generate; this is the foundation of the "Magic Formula." If you keep in mind with modesty that you are an energy converter and can create your dream world, it means you are ready to start applying and practicing each principle.

All of the seven principles are equally important. If something is not clear to you, read and listen to it as many times as you need. What I do when I don't understand a word or a concept, is to take notes. Later on, when I review my notes, I suddenly get the idea. What I didn't understand before will then make sense to me. The good thing is that you can apply your knowledge as you go along; you don't need to wait until you finish the whole book.

The book is divided into several chapters with an exercise at the end of each chapter for you to start practicing and applying every step of what you learn. After you read the book one time, I suggest that you listen to the audio CD recording too.

It should take no more than a month for you to start manifesting your dreams and wishes. Depending on each individual it could vary a few days more or less. Some people have created some or most of their dreams to reach their happiness in as little as one month. However, as time passes by, and during the process of this creation, other dreams will arise for you to create. Time has no limits and your dreams shouldn't be limited either.

I hope you enjoy this journey to the world where your dreams become real. With certainty there is not a specific time for you to master the art of creating your happiness, simply enjoy the journey and remember: it is totally up to you and how soon you want to embark and sail your boat toward the desired port.

Wright

Does it mean that I will never be sad, mad, or depressed if I learn to apply the formula?

Talisman

Whenever you feel sad, upset, depressed, or betrayed, remember there is a book someone wrote especially for you to you read and that it will surely make you feel better. It will help you focus your attention in the beauty of life and the treasures around you. Just learn the seven magic principles of my formula and apply them in your everyday life. You will see everything from a different perspective, including the moments that used to make you depressed, mad, anxious, angry, and any other feeling hard for you to manage.

I believe that one of the reasons people become depressed is because of the lack of spiritual nourishment. We must remember that our essence as human beings is spiritual and natural. All of our attention usually goes to our physical being—eating, working out, dressing, work, diets, vitamins, intellect, and so much more. However, how do we nourish our spirit? This formula and its seven principles nourish your spirit. The formula gives you practices and suggestions for soul and spirit exercises.

Dr. Deepak Chopra, author and great visionary, said that what people with addictions of some kind really lack or need more of is spirituality. I agree with him—his words are profound. We all need food for the soul.

I would also like to give credit to the precious woman through whose actions I was shown the precious meaning of love and gratefulness. She is my paternal grandmother, Mama Mia—I mentioned her earlier. She is now a spirit. When I was only nineteen years old and married with two beautiful baby girls, I was going through a very "dark night" of my soul (Thomas Moore refers to this kind of experience in his book *Dark Nights*). I had just recently discovered my husband's infidelity and was in despair. Mama Mia was visiting me and I told her I wanted to die because I was so unlucky and miserable.

She was silent and then she said to me, "Hijita, what in the world are you saying? You should never feel sad or unlucky! Just look around you. Look at all that has been given to you. Look at me! I love you more than anything in this life. Do you see your beautiful healthy little girls? They need you more than anything on earth, and they need you to be happy. Do you see the flowers, the birds, the shining sun, the luminous moon, and the beautiful blossoming nature around you?" She hugged me and kissed me. "Never forget how fortunate you are." Her beautiful lesson made me realize that even when things go wrong, our wonderful world is full of things that bring us happiness.

Wright

Can you assure readers that after learning the seven magic principles they will be happy?

Talisman

I can assure one thing—reading *The Art of Creating Your Happiness* and applying the seven magic principles are two different things. Readers will know in theory the art of creating happiness, but they must practice it. My mission is to share that method; but some may find it more challenging than others. For specific concerns, feel free to contact me please do so at: Rozhy.com.

Wright

I understand your book is coming out very soon. How will we know when it will be available and where?

Talisman

It will come out very soon, before the end of this year—2008. My audio recording is already available through my Web site and I will let everybody know when my book is out and where it's available.

Wright

Well, what a great conversation. You've made some great points about happiness, and I'm sure your life's journey has taught you a lot about being happy. It sounds like it's working.

Talisman

Yes it is. It is very fulfilling and motivating.

Wright

I really do appreciate the time you've spent answering all these questions. I really did learn a lot and I thank you for taking the time to talk with me today.

Talisman

Thank you very much, David. It was really a pleasure to be able to express my feelings. I feel fortunate to be able to transmit them to all of you.

Wright

Today we've been talking with Rozhy Talisman. She is a universal motivator, a sales trainer, and a happiness coach from Dallas, Texas. I think she's got some great points.

Rozhy, thank you so much for being with us today on *Leading the Way to Success.*

Talisman

Thank you very much, David.

About the Author

Rozhy Talisman was born in Guadalajara, Mexico, and currently resides in Dallas, Texas. She gave birth to five beautiful children whose names are Connie, Amy, Veronica, Gabriela, and Ivan. She had two great men in her life, her father, Leo, and her first husband, Octa. Today, she shares her life with her husband and friend, Steve. Her spiritual avatar was her grandmother, Mama Mia. Her musical inspiration is her mother, Irene, and as an author and poet her aunt Rosario.

She holds a bachelor's degree in Business and Real Estate. She is Vice President of Sales and Business Development for a national corporation. She is a motivational speaker and a sales and happiness coach.

Rozhy is author of the book, *The Art of Creating Your Happiness.* Among others, she developed a program for sales and marketing called, "Be Happy, Sell More." Her plans for the future are to help everyone who wishes achieve happiness. Her definition of success is: "Happiness is Success." "We all can use a little bit of this happiness," she says.

Rozhy Talisman
3142 Royal Gable Drive
Dallas, TX 75229
469-231-4048
www.rozhy.com
www.createyourhappiness.com

Rozhy Talisman

Chapter 8

Bill Reed

David Wright (Wright)

Today we're talking with William A. Reed, PhD, who is called "Dr. Bill" by his clients and colleagues. He is the Founder and Executive Director of Coach Dynamics LLC. He formed Coach Dynamics in 2001 to help business owners and executives improve performance and satisfaction on a personal, professional, and organizational level. Dr. Bill offers clients more than thirty-five years of corporate and management experience. As a teacher and public speaker, Dr. Bill motivates his individual and his corporate clients to identify the root cause of their problems rather than focusing on temporary fixes, distractions, or denial tactics. Dr. Bill has worked with many major corporations, family owned businesses, and individuals in the areas of sales, management, leadership, work-life balance, and organizational and personal performance. He holds a bachelor's degree in Science and Technology, a master's degree in Science of Management and a PhD in Management Performance and Leadership. Currently Dr. Bill is Chairperson of Leadership and Organizational Development at Capella University School of Business and Technology where he works with PhD applicants and their leadership research.

Bill, welcome to *Leading the Way to Success.*

Bill Reed (Reed)

Good afternoon David, it's nice to be with you.

Wright

So how are the leadership perceptions of today and tomorrow different from the leadership perspectives of the past?

Reed

Well, I think, David that comes down to two categories of perception. One is from our leaders and the other is from those who are led. We've all heard the expression that our perceptions become our reality; at this time I think that this has never been more true than when we speak about leadership. We have many different perceptions of leadership because leadership means different things to different people.

On a global level we see areas of world communities being developed that we haven't seen in the past and different alliances being created in partnerships—in business and in government. We've experienced in the last twenty to thirty years generational differences, specifically, the impact of generational differences.

Overlying generational considerations, in addition to the date when we were born, is the issue of different eras that we've been living through. We've come through the industrial era, the Vietnam Era, the technology era, and the 9/11 era. All of these periods have deeply affected how we look at people and how we think of leadership. In essence, we are viewing leadership, and the world, from our own lived experiences and individually lived systems.

Taking a view from the follower perspective, those who are led see leadership as different. I think we see now a much more concentrated effort and focus on the issues of moral values and ethical considerations. We need to question leaders more—we need to question their abilities and their motives more.

Another major change that has draped the current perception of leadership is just how much we're aware of the issue of human behavior as it applies to leadership situations. A historical view of leadership would indicate a major turn in looking at human behaviors in a study that we've done many, many years ago in Hawthorne, Illinois, at the GE plant. This study later became known as the Hawthorne Studies. Leaders began to understand that there is a human behavior issue to this. Further, most would agree that an increase in creativity will be part of any future leadership definition.

Traditional leadership paths, along with the traditional leadership providers are slowly drying up; not delivering the needed leaders to match the demands of business and management leadership needs. We will see many untraditional styles of leadership emerging in order to meet demands placed on leaders. We are seeing traditional paradigms of leadership development dying, which is initiating the need for new ideas and approaches to filling the leadership needs.

I also see that the loyalty levels of leaders—devotion to one organization—slowly diminishing. Leaders are more often hired by contract arrangement for key leadership positions rather than by climbing the corporate ladder. This is creating a "just in time" leadership model that by design or circumstance is emerging in many organizations.

I think all of this really combines to acknowledge the fact that we are in constant change when we talk about leadership. As we explore more aspects of leadership we seem to learn more, and yet we uncover more that we still need to learn.

Wright

Can there be a "perfect leader" to meet our increasing needs and demands?

Reed

The question of a perfect leader could be more of an ideal than a reality. If we could identify a perfect leader we'd probably be able to define leadership more comprehensively. If a perfect leader were possible, I think we'd be able to model it—we'd be able to shape, measure, and diagram it. I don't think we're capable of doing those things to a significant degree. There are many ingredients or components to leaders and leadership that just varies so often.

First there are situational issues—situations require different leadership skills. While many of the skills are common to many areas, they just simply foster themselves and develop more need in certain situations. Some areas require vigor, empowerment, encouragement, high level of trust, and a high level of ethical standards.

It just seems to me that to create a perfect leader is just not possible, particularly as we move ahead in business in our world society where we seem to be globalizing in so many areas. I just don't think that one perfect leader would be able to solve all that needs to be solved. Just as we spoke about perceptions (and the definitions of a perfect leader is a perception), we may have a perfect leader for a given situation—a situation in a given time—but I don't know how much further than that we could really define the term "perfect leader."

Wright

So what skills and abilities are needed to lead in a virtual global organization where people may not ever have seen or been to the organization they're working for?

Reed

As we progress into the 2020s and 2030s this is going to be a major area of opportunity for leaders and those of us who study leadership. I think many of the skills and components of leaders will remain the same. These will include areas such as determination, vision, being able to guide and direct, and to mentor. I think a couple of the areas that will require additional learning and additional concentration is that of communication, and not simply in the sense of verbal language but in all levels of communication.

For example, people often are often challenged now to communicate online. Online communication sacrifices the benefit of face-to-face—reading people's faces and hearing the tone of their message. This is something that leaders and all communicators are going to have to learn to do as we get more and more into a technology based communication pattern.

Additionally, I think understanding cultural issues in global environments and being able to mix cultures until they understand the objectives must be an aspect of future leaders' capabilities. Many studies have been done already about cultures regarding individuals and organizations that have come to the United States and bought businesses.

There are U.S. companies that have gone abroad and one of the major challenges they faced initially is that of cultural indoctrination. Cultural diversity is a major issue and it's going to be increase in importance as we globalize.

I conclude that we will see a significant increase of collaborative styles of leadership—bringing together multiple areas of expertise to manage a given managerial issue. Alert and idea-driven leaders should be in demand by multi-national organizations, as well as in the smaller entrepreneurial, and start-up, organizations.

We need to understand that the integration of those who lead in a global organization can be challenging and what is good in one location may not work in another. We read often that in many companies today we're already experiencing this challenge in trying to identify what is needed and what is not needed.

Finally, I envision that future leaders will need to be more teacher-oriented in their styles, enabling their teams to learn from each member and reaching consensus on extremely complicated issues.

Wright

So is leadership an archaic topic that will be replaced by another term that focuses on some other pertinent aspect of how people work together?

Reed

David, I think we're going to be talking about leadership for a long time to come. It may take on different shapes and it may take on different requirements, but I think the topic itself is here to stay. As we look at leadership, we may change how we define it and what we think of it, but I think we have to understand that change is a constant and as we change, leadership requirements will change appropriately. Perhaps the role of leadership will change, maybe we won't have a single leader in charge of a company anymore; we may have team leadership. Leadership may be comprised of groups that now comprehensively manage through team efforts. This is already happening, and we see it in various project management functions. There are other considerations as well, as we consider the validity of talking about leadership and if there's something new coming.

Bill Reed

I think what will change is how we basically define our leaders, what we're looking for in our leaders, and what we expect from our leaders. I think some of the basic individual skills that have been well discussed and studied over the years will remain. Different skill requirements may emerge, but I think the topic of leadership will be here for a long time, based on the fact that we haven't defined it that well. Defining leadership is as difficult as trying to hit a moving and changing target.

David, we need to be aware of the macro view as well as the micro view of leadership. On the macro level, birth rates in our country are diminishing. Baby Boomers are starting to retire, leaving the pool of potential leaders dwindling. Who will replace these leaders? The next generation of leaders appears to have different goals, perhaps not matching the norms established by the Boomers. What affect will this have? Research is needed in this area to forecast the needs these leaders will expect in return for their expertise. An example might be the research showing that Generation X and Next Generation folks want more freedom to enjoy living—more time for fun. How will this play out when faced with future demands of organizations?

Wright

How can a business be successful without strong leadership?

Reed

It is my belief that a business can be successful without strong leadership on a very limited or short-term basis. As a member of a senior management team, we were in such a company. This company was basically surviving on momentum and desire to succeed. It did not necessarily have strong leadership, which meant to me that the company itself was not going to sustain itself through the long-term, which years later it did not. You can always grow through momentum; many small companies do this successfully. When you look at the long-term, I think strong leadership—leaders who have a vision, who can understand goals, and understand markets and conditions—will determine the companies that will be more successful in the long-term. Without strong leaders, the sustainability of a business would be in question and it will probably not achieve the potential otherwise available to organizations with stronger leadership.

Wright

With the advent of Level 5 and transformative leadership, where is leadership headed and what will it look like in twenty years?

Reed

We can look back twenty years ago and say, "Well, I didn't know we'd be where we are today." It's fairly difficult to project twenty years ahead. I think the learning that we've acquired from the Level 5 work, transformational leadership studies (and many, many others for that matter) are contributing to how we will be able to better handle the leadership needs of the future.

One of the main considerations that I've experienced in the mixture of my academic work and my actual corporate work is that as leadership progresses through the ranks it changes. We're experiencing a transition from older leaders to a younger group of leaders who are emerging from the Generation X group. These people see the world differently, and they've been brought up differently. Basically they are individual products of their own system. By that I mean the influences they have had—who they grew up with, where they grew up, how they were raised by their parents, and so on—affects their thinking and perspective. This will all change as the continuum moves forward through the years, it's an interesting challenge.

In the last twenty years we've seen that older people have had to report to younger leaders. This was an initial shock maybe twenty or twenty-five years ago, but now it's more easily managed than it was then.

It should also be understood that the very nature of work is quickly changing, placing additional demands on leadership styles. Shifting worker population, changing workplace dynamics, commitment of an organization to allocate resources to training future management will all affect future leadership.

I think it is important to recognize that the current approaches to managerial development and designing organizational effectiveness are slowly becoming less and less meaningful and new approaches will be needed to achieve increased development and effectiveness. Leadership in the future will also require a new educational sophistication whereby

127

leaders will have an established plan to match the historical leadership learning of the past to the needs and demands of current and future leadership requirements.

So this learning curve that we're experiencing through issues like Level 5, transformational, and a host of others studies that have been done, will really add to how leaders are groomed, how they're selected, how they're respected, and how they will manage companies as we move ahead into the next twenty and thirty years.

Wright

As leaders, face new and demanding challenges. How can leaders embrace these challenges and successfully move their organizations forward?

Reed

The true characteristics of leader are evidenced by people who can recognize the change as it begins or before it actually happens. Leaders who exhibit these characteristics can invigorate their management teams to gather the momentum necessary to accept these changes and challenges and to make the proper decisions. There's no easy way out when it comes to being a leader in today's public companies. These demanding jobs require a lot of attention. This is why I feel that leadership will be distributed and include many people in the organization rather than historically the one main person. I think leadership teams are the emerging factor and I think that's how this will be adjusted as we move ahead for companies to remain successful.

Wright

Do you think a manager also needs to be a leader?

Reed

This is an age-old question, David. Is a manager a leader or is a leader a manager? I think a manager has to be a leader to some level in all areas. A basic definition is that the manager is in charge of the operational aspect of the corporation. Managers have to get the job done. Conversely, leaders create the vision and set the goals to move forward, but at some point in that spectrum they have to connect and understand just what is being done and what needs to be done. So to that degree I think that a manager is a leader.

I think managers must also understand the operational vision of the company. I don't think they can mange successfully without that. They also must understand both the customer's perspective and upper management's perspective; that requires leadership skills. The time needed to learn that varies. I have worked with managers who are very, very good leaders, and I have worked with managers who are better at operational management. So it is a mixture—it involves more than one aspect. But basically, to address the issue, I think managers, to some degree, are leaders because they have people they must guide and move forward within the organization and they must meet the goals set forth.

I would think that the answer to this question comes right down to the capacity of one person/manager to become a single integrated person who represents the needs of a manager and a leader in a given situation. In this situation, a manager is a leader. In most cases, however, I feel the needs and demands of the manager and the leader are separate and unique. This does, of course, bring up the newer concept of "followership."

Wright

Do you think anyone who desires to lead actually can become a leader?

Reed

I think there are many people who have the characteristics and skills necessary to be leaders. Some of these people may not want to be in a leadership position, but for those people who truly want to lead and to move on I think there's a good chance. Simply possessing the desire to lead is one of the most important ingredients to becoming a leader. The motivation factors to becoming a leader are many. These factors basically fall into two categories in my opinion—extrinsic and intrinsic motivators. The extrinsic are external motivators such as perception of friends, relative status in their social groups, and perhaps status in the community. The intrinsic values include self-worth, self-value, desire to achieve a goal, and so on.

Bill Reed

I think leadership can be learned. If you have certain characteristics that are commonly associated with leadership, you can identify them, build on them, work on them, and improve them. I think that most people who want to lead can lead in given situations. Will they ever achieve high status or become President of the United States? Maybe not, but they could be a good leader within their own sphere of influence—in their own communities and in their own environments.

Another perspective is that most organizational positions in the future are designed for college-educated individuals. Will this affect the capacity for anyone to lead? I think so. Future leaders will need to satisfy a variety of foundational skills and abilities in order to grow into a leadership role.

Wright

You've talked a lot about technology in relationship to leadership; would you tell our readers how you see technology affecting leaders and leadership styles?

Reed

My perception on the major affect of technology is that the good leader recognizes technology as a tool. I think leaders can obviously use technology to their advantage. We spoke earlier about globalization and we've talked about communication. A leader can use technology in those areas. The ability of a leader to successfully use technology really comes down to the point of interaction and the ability to integrate that technology into the organization and into the leadership structure. I mentioned that communication is an important part of that. I think goals and vision need to be built around the concept and the use of technology. Today we see technology as an intrinsic part of management in companies, so I don't think there is really any way to separate it out as we move forward. The ability to use it, and more importantly the ability to understand the affect of technology, is probably the most significant aspect that a leader would need to consider as he or she moves a company forward.

The future leader will need to be totally engaged with technology. A strong understanding of the benefits and drawbacks that technology provides and the ability to effectively use technology are important aspects of future leaders.

Wright

How do you view the relationship between leadership and followership?

Reed

Followership is really a relatively new and it is an area just starting to receive serious research efforts. I am working with PhD learners now who are doing studies on followership. I had the opportunity many years ago to meet and speak with Peter Drucker and he had a lot to say about followership.

I had just completed many years of study of leadership and I went to a presentation of his. He said that followership is the next most important issue management is going to have to understand. One of the important aspects of being a good leader and being a good follower is the ability to be a change agent. I think that's a common denominator for both. I think people choose to be followers rather than leaders perhaps for a number of reasons—less stress, work-life balance issues, or preference to being a good executor of the vision of the leader. So I think a lot of this is yet to be studied and fully understood. Some of the things a follower would have to do is, of course (as I mentioned) to understand the vision, understand the goals, and to be able to work within the framework that the leader sets up for that company or organization.

Organizations benefit from solid and devoted followers. The integration of the followership concepts into a followership/leadership integrated theory will be an interesting new paradigm over the next decade or so. Of particular importance is the relative effectiveness that followers contribute to the leadership of an organization—an interesting area of study.

I am confident that as we go through the next fifteen or twenty years, the subject of followership is going to be a highly studied area, an area that will help people understand their position, to see where they are relative to the organization, and to allow them to be respected wherever they are in the organization, as they contribute to the growth and forward movement of that company.

Wright

It's been said (and I've read this in a particular book) that 98 percent of the workforce are followers and 2 percent are leaders. The author of the book said that most people misunderstand this—they think that somehow the 2 percent are better than the 98 percent. But the point he was making is that each chose—the 2 percent chose to be leaders and the 98 percent chose to be followers. Do you think that's true?

Reed

I don't believe that any given 2 percent of any organization is better than any given 98 percent of an organization. The 2 percent may not be better, but they might have worked harder to achieve more than the other 98 percent.

I believe that you could have an organization where 2 percent are the leaders and 98 percent are good followers. In this case, you probably have an excellent organizational structure and an excellent organizational culture.

This reminds me very much of the foundations of Servant Leadership as created by Robert Greenleaf back in the 1960s. A strong followership component of an organization would probably be a very strong culture, a positive work environment, and consist of many contributing work groups.

I would think that anyone who thought that the 2 percent are "better" have probably misread the situation. It is totally possible that the 2 percent actually took specific initiatives to become part of the 2 percent leader group.

Wright

So how much power does a leader need to be effective?

Reed

The issue of "how much power" is a pretty tough question. The issue of power comes in two areas: that of real power and that of perceived power. The leader would need the power to bring about the goals and vision of the company, so whatever relative level of power would accomplish that goal is probably what the leader would need.

There is a difference here too of the type of organization and the type of power needed. In a business organization, the leader might need more power; however, if you looked at an organization like a church or a social group, perhaps the power would be less necessary in those situations. One of the things that would have to be considered when speaking of power is the balance of power—the balance that would bring about the results of positive change.

It's always an interesting discussion when talking about power. When I instructed in a master's level course, we used an analysis based on Adolph Hitler. Adolph Hitler was a leader. He was perhaps not a leader that we would all aspire to be or be with, but by the terms that we normally associate with leadership and the characteristics we attribute to leaders, he was one. However, he had supreme power—at least for a time—and that would be a corruptive type power. There are powers that stimulate a much better result and aim at the good of the people. The concept of power in leadership requires a very delicate balance. We've seen in the newspapers over the last several years that the misuse of power can lead to disastrous results for organizations and losses for members of those organizations.

Powers, and the ability of the leader to lead, coupled with appropriate communication are key ingredients to the delicate balance of leadership, power, and positive results.

Wright

So do you think that leaders have to be exceptional communicators?

Reed

I certainly do agree on the need for effective communication among leaders. I think it's a cornerstone of being a leader. History has shown us over the years the importance and critical nature of communication. One could conduct a study and find that most perceived good leaders were also masters at communicating their visions, goals, and ambitions to their organizations. The people who are able to communicate their vision and goals and clearly define them so that their organizations can follow them simply seem to have a strong advantage over those who can't.

I mentioned this earlier when we talked about virtual communication and virtual companies. It is an unbelievable change when you communicate virtually than when you communicate one-on-one in a face-to-face environment. Management must really understand that communication is a cornerstone. I don't think that this is a new problem. I think this is something that has been on the table and on the concern list for many organizations for many, many, years. It is extremely important for managers and leaders to have the ability to clearly communicate and to have the ability to put forth the necessary ingredients so that everyone in the organization including customer, suppliers, and employees understands. Clear communication is important for the improvement, forward motion, and the success of every company.

Also consider that as organizations continue to grow globally, communication across cultures and dialects become ever increasing skills. Not simply the spoken word, but the implication of nonverbal communication as well.

Wright

What a great conversation Bill I really appreciate you taking all this time today to answer these questions. I have certainly learned a lot and I'm sure that our readers will.

Reed

Well thank you David for having me and I've enjoyed the conversation also.

Wright

Today we've been talking with William A. Reed, PhD, whose clients and colleagues call him Dr. Bill. He formed Coach Dynamics in 2001 to help business owners and executives improve performance and satisfaction on a personal, professional, and organizational level. He motivates his individual corporate clients to identify the root cause of their problems, rather than focusing on temporary fixes, distractions, or denial tactics.

Dr. Bill, thank you so much for being with us today on *Leading the Way to Success.*

Reed

Thank you, David, thank you very much.

About the Author

William A. Reed, PhD is called "Dr. Bill" by his clients and colleagues. He is the Founder and Executive Director of Coach Dynamics LLC. He formed Coach Dynamics in 2001 to help business owners and executives improve performance and satisfaction on a personal, professional, and organizational level. Dr. Bill offers clients more than thirty-five years of corporate and management experience. As a teacher and public speaker, Dr. Bill motivates his individual and his corporate clients to identify the root cause of their problems rather than focusing on temporary fixes, distractions, or denial tactics. Dr. Bill has worked with many major corporations, family owned businesses, and individuals in the areas of sales, management, leadership, work-life balance, and organizational and personal performance. He holds a bachelor's degree in Science and Technology, a master's degree in Science of Management and a PhD in Management Performance and Leadership. Currently Dr. Bill is Chairperson of Leadership and Organizational Development at Capella University School of Business and Technology where he works with PhD applicants and their leadership research.

Bill Reed, Ph.D.
#174, 1133 Bal Harbor Blvd., Suite 1139
Punta Gorda, FL 33950
732.793.4200
wreed@infionline.net
bill.reed@Capella.edu
www.coachdynamics.com

Chapter 9

Gerry Myers

David Wright (Wright)

Today we're talking with Gerry Myers, CEO of Advisory Link. Gerry brings more than fifteen years experience in helping businesses market and sell products more effectively to women, as well as assisting them in the creation of programs to recruit, retain, and promote women within their organizations. She is an international speaker, trainer, and consultant who has written articles and been featured and/or quoted as an authority on women in publications such as *The New York Times, The Financial Post, The Dallas Business Journal, Dealer Magazine, MarketingProf.com,* and *American Demographics.* A pioneer in the women's market and the first author to publish a book on the subject in 1994, Gerry's client roster includes MassMutual Financial Group, New York Life Insurance Company, Toyota Motor Sales, Ford Motor Company, and ClubCorp.

Gerry, welcome to *Leading the Way to Success.*

Gerry Myers (Myers)

Thank you, David.

Wright

To begin, what would you say are differences in men's and women's leadership styles, if any?

Myers

There are a number of differences between the genders, as well as between individuals of the same sex. Even though both men and women have certain traits that are more prevalent to their sex, gender attributes are on a continuum. This means that if you put the most masculine traits at one end and the most feminine traits on the other end, while one end would have more men and the other end have more women, there would be men and women at all spots on the continuum.

Below are a few examples of differences between men and women that impact their communication and leadership with each other on the job:

Women
- Tend to adopt a democratic leadership style,
- Are centric-related and less hierarchical,
- Encourage participation and share power and information to instill confidence and self-worth in others,
- Are collaborative and seek consensus,
- Consider more options and details when making decisions and therefore often take longer to make decisions,
- "Toot their horn" much less,
- Aren't recognized as quickly for their accomplishments and thus don't move up the leadership ladder as fast.

Men
- Are more inclined to adapt a formal, direct command and control style,
- Are more hierarchical and less inclusive,
- See information as power. As a general rule, males share only as much information as they need to get the job done. They like autonomy,
- Tend to be more confrontational and competitive,
- Consider less options and consult with fewer people, thus making quicker decisions,
- Boast more about their accomplishments,
- Tend to get more promotions and raises as a result of singing their own praises.

Wright

So what are some ways women can augment their leadership skills?

Myers

Women can develop proficiency in many business areas by attending seminars and conferences, mastering necessary skills, reading books, joining peer coaching organizations, and taking on challenging new assignments. Organizations are looking for leaders who:

- Think outside boundaries,
- Translate business objectives into sound operating plans,
- Accept reasonable risk, and
- Bring teams together to reach established goals.

While all these steps are important, women who want to experience greater success need a mentor and/or coach. It's easier to understand the culture and move up in a corporation when someone else is helping you. Men have known this for years. When top male executives spot a male rising star in their organizations, they take him under their wings, introduce him around, and provide timely insights and advice. Occasionally a man will realize the value to the organization of a female rising star and mentor her, but this happens much less often than men mentoring men, even though men can be very effective mentors to women. Unfortunately, there aren't enough women in high-level positions to mentor the up-and-coming women in most organizations. As a result, they often struggle more because they don't receive the same guidance as their male peers. Mentors help aspiring employees build business relationships and navigate their careers.

Women need to take responsibility for letting their supervisors know they have a desire to advance. Women believe hard work will provide the results they want, but it usually won't. To compound the problem, management often makes assumptions about women that are erroneous. For instance: she does not want to work long hours, she doesn't want to travel, or she doesn't want a foreign assignment. If women are interested in promotions, they need to make sure the appropriate people know their career goals.

Wright

Why should an organization devote resources to advance women's leadership potential? In other words, WIIFM (what's in it for me)?

Myers

The main reason corporations need to invest in women's leadership development is to be able to tap into 100 percent of the talent pool, rather than just 50 percent. When interviewing and considering their employment options, women look at the makeup of upper management. They want to know who is leading this company. Are there women in upper management? Do they have a chance to move up in this organization? If their assessment is *no,* then they won't be interested in going to work for that business. Women will open their own companies or go to work for a rival firm.

To remain healthy in both good and bad economies, companies must hire top talent from all ethnic backgrounds and age ranges. This will ensure a diverse workforce that will contribute various perspectives on issues, products, and services, as well as put businesses in closer alignment with the demographics of their customers and community. After hiring talented women, the company needs to let them know they are an integral part of the organization by providing leadership and career development opportunities. These efforts can include career coaches, external peer coaching groups, and internal women's initiatives that support female employees.

Wright

Why are businesses just beginning to see the relationship between leadership development of female employees and marketing their products more successfully to women?

Myers

With the retiring Boomers, there's a real "brain drain" on corporations. They are beginning to wonder how they're going to fill critical positions. With women opening their own companies at twice the rate of the overall population, corporations that want to stay current and grow are realizing the need to be more generous and genuine when filling key positions.

Smart firms know they need to attract and retain the best of the best, and that includes more women.

In addition to their employment practices, companies are focusing a lot more dollars on marketing and selling to women. This decision is *not* based on political correctness, but on sound business basics—women control the money. They spend eighty-five cents of every dollar. In virtually all industries, they make more than 50 percent of the purchases, including automotive products, electronics, sports gear and equipment, healthcare, and internet sales. If businesses aren't marketing their products and services successfully to women, they're losing out on billions of dollars annually. Marketing and selling successfully to women is really about profitability, growth, and sometimes even survival.

Wright

How do developing leadership and advancement opportunities for female employees affect the company's market share?

Myers

Companies that advance women into management positions have a better perspective on their customers' wants, needs, and buying habits. They also bring skills and talents to organizations that male executives may not have. Women are generally viewed as better listeners, more honest, collaborative, and detail-oriented. Additionally, hiring and advancing women impacts business revenue and market share because many women prefer buying from organizations that are female and family friendly.

Furthermore, women provide a very different viewpoint on product design. A few years ago, in an attempt to help engineers at Ford Motor Company understand some of the challenges women face, they were asked to put paper clips on their nails so they could get the feel of long fingernails. By hiring more women in design, these types of challenges were minimized.

Green has also become a huge issue, and while it is important to both genders, women are much more conscious of the environment. Social responsibility and cause marketing are both important to women. Therefore, it is a good business strategy to have women in positions to make decisions on these issues. It is a misnomer that price is paramount with women. They often look beyond the product and the price to other issues that are important to them. As a result, women in leadership positions will continue to play a critical role in the growth of a company's market share and revenue.

Wright

So if a business hires good female employees, all of their marketing to women problems will be solved?

Myers

No. One of the biggest mistakes I see companies make is they assume all women can market to women based strictly on their gender with total disregard for their abilities. That's just not the case. Executives would never presume all their male employees have marketing expertise. Employee skills are diverse; some are attorneys, others are accountants, and a number are on the manufacturer's front lines. They each have specific skills, training, and experiences that enable them to do their jobs.

To market to women successfully, establishments need to focus on creating both external and internal Women's Initiatives that have set goals and measurable results. These types of programs generally are best managed in tandem by a high level executive and an outside consultant who specialize in marketing to women.

Wright

Why would companies want to allocate significant dollars and create programs that focus on the women's market rather than continuing to do business as usual?

Myers

That's an interesting question because I've always wondered *why wouldn't they?* Women spend 85 percent of every dollar, whereas men spend only 15 percent. Women:

- Buy 51 percent of all electronics, which accounts for more than $55 billion,
- Purchase more than 50 percent of all automotive vehicles totaling more than $83 billion in revenue,

- Make more than 51 percent of online purchases,
- Initiate 80 percent or more than $70 billion of all home improvement purchases,
- Make 80 percent of healthcare decisions,
- Influence or purchase 91 percent of homes, and
- Even buy nearly 80 percent of NFL products.

Women are purchasing agents for businesses, for their families, and for themselves. During the second decade of this century, women will control approximately 60 percent of all the wealth in the United States. So marketing to women is not something companies should do because it's politically correct, but because there is a sound business case for doing it.

The most destructive marketing myth that affects how companies allocate their marketing dollars and create advertising campaigns is their fear that they will lose sales to men if they focus on selling to women. That hasn't proven to be the case. In fact, the opposite is true. Carefully crafted and implemented programs increase male clients as well as female because men have liked the changes women have suggested.

When companies are totally off base in their marketing to women tactics and think the solution is to make the product pink, neither men nor women are going to buy it. In the beginning, the main and oftentimes the only marketing to women strategy companies had was to make their products pink. Pink is a color, not a marketing strategy. When companies *really* know what women want in the products and services they buy, then they make meaningful changes and enhance their customer base and revenue.

It doesn't matter if you are a hotel, drycleaner, auto dealership, or electronics retailer, when you look at what women want, and make correct and carefully calculated changes, women become loyal customers, and so do men.

Wright

What can an organization do to increase both its employment and customer base of women who are centers of influence?

Gerry Myers

Myers

No marketing effort should stand alone. Marketing to women needs to be integrated into a company's business plan and marketing strategies. Recruiting, retaining, and promoting women require the same commitment from top management. It is a dual effort because businesses must implement programs both internally and externally. It is important that those in charge of executing the plans be held accountable. Adequate resources have to be allocated to ensure success of the project. This means both dollars and people.

It is often more effective and cost efficient to hire an outside consultant to help drive the initiative. Companies such as Advisory Link that specialize in this arena already know what works and what doesn't. These ventures, which don't have to be expensive, can be funded by reallocating existing marketing and human resource budgets.

As part of a multi-faceted approach, corporations can engage keynote speakers or panels for important management meetings. By talking about women's initiatives and making the business case for why the company is focusing its efforts on marketing, selling, hiring, and promoting women, they will receive buy-in from key players in the organization. Consultants can assist with this as well as provide sales training. While it is important to have management support, it is equally important that employees who have the most contact with customers understand and internalize the process. Explaining how much wealth women control and how much buying power they have will assist everyone in reaching stated goals. Understanding gender and generational differences in communication and leadership styles, as well as buying patterns, will make the cultural transitions more seamless. Additionally, consultants can help develop an internal women's networking support group that mentors and supports new women and rising stars.

Externally, the single best vehicle a corporation can have is a Women's Advisory Board. Companies that have had Women's Advisory Boards (WABs) have increased revenue significantly, produced more award-winning salespeople, had better employee retention, helped women develop their leadership skills, and hired more diversity in their staffs. These companies thrive because of the caliber of women brought in to help them.

A WAB works with you to develop strategies for marketing and selling more effectively and for recruiting and retaining employees. They contribute strategic solutions on how to hire women more successfully, including: how to provide them with leadership development and the right connections, where to find quality women, and where to place ads. In other words, they become ambassadors for your company. It's an extraordinary program, but like any other process, it has pitfalls. If you don't put the right people on the Board, communicate a clear mission, allocate an appropriate budget, and develop measurable goals to check your progress, you will fail to get the benefits from a WAB that are possible. An outside consultant with a proven track record in this area can help you avoid these mistakes and ensure your success.

Wright

Why are Women's Advisory Boards so powerful? What results have companies had that have incorporated Women's Advisory Boards into their business plans?

Myers

When more awareness of the importance of women is created, processes are revisited, programs refined, and good things happen. Corporations are slowly making their culture more female-friendly, R&D and salespeople are starting to grasp the nuances in gender differences, and women are beginning to feel their strength. Companies are attending conferences that focus on marketing to women and are appointing women executives to handle initiatives. Along with the results from years of hiring speakers and consultants and reading numerous books on the topic, one of the best tools a company can have in its arsenal is a Women's Advisory Board. Because you're asking your present and targeted customers directly what they want, you get clear, concise, effective solutions and ideas that will avoid costly errors.

A WAB is more than a focus group. It becomes committed to you, your products, and your services. They not only provide invaluable, honest advice and recommendations, but also connect you to their network of very influential women in the community. In addition, they are flexible and can be customized for your specific needs. WABs can be geographically, academically, economically, and demographically diverse.

The results have been impressive:

- MassMutual Financial Group's Women's Advisory Board program produced sales that were 146 percent of their sales quotas in agencies that had WABs. Additionally, they helped increase recruitment, retention, and promotion of women.
- The Wyndham Hotel increased women business travelers by 59 percent after forming a Women's Advisory Board. One of its initiatives was the creation of its highly successful *Women on Their Way*® program.
- ClubCorp increased its membership with women and involved more women in its club activities.
- Avis Rent-a-Car created a Women's Advisory Board to continually monitor the pulse of female travelers to make sure they were offering the things women wanted.
- New York Life Insurance Company won an award for its innovative actions with Women's Advisory Boards.

The ROI of all Women's Advisory Boards has been more recognition, more clients, more competent hires, and more revenue.

Wright

You mentioned a lot of things companies can do to elevate women within their organization and increase their sales to women. How did you get involved in this endeavor?

Myers

When I started focusing on the women's market in the early nineties, companies literally did not even realize there was a women's market. They didn't understand that female consumers bought differently, thought differently, and had to be sold to differently.

As a single, professional woman running a company, I needed a new car. I went to six different dealerships; five treated me poorly. They used high-pressured tactics, told me "not to worry my pretty little head about the finances," and asked me to bring my husband in. The experience was awful, but I realized the need for education and training in this area.

Today there is much more awareness and this is one of the things we have done that I am very proud of because it creates a win-win for both the company and consumer.

As Advisory Link evolved, it became clear to me that I could provide an even greater service by creating Women's Advisory Boards that were customized for each client to provide them with an army of women to help them, not just me. When women are engaged and tell their extensive networks of colleagues, friends, and family about it, it helps build a company's business.

In addition to Advisory Link's Women's Advisory Board program, we also offer a wide range of training, speaking, and consulting programs. As a result, our clients have seen:

- Increases in revenue,
- New customers leading to larger databases,
- Less turnover in employees,
- More quality recruitment, and
- Better retention.

A company doesn't have to find new money to gain the advantages of our programs. As I said earlier, businesses can reallocate a portion of the money that is presently being spent on traditional advertising and get much better results with women consumers.

Advisory Link has helped companies reach new markets they haven't been able to cultivate, such as the military, ethnic communities, and school districts. We have helped make sure new female managers or salespersons had mentors and business skills to ensure their success. We have provided more visibility in the community for our clients. Businesses have won awards, increased revenue, hired more talented women, and in general, were more successful as a result of our programs and training. That's why I'm so passionate about what we do.

Wright

Are women a homogeneous market where I can develop a "one program fits all" posture?

Myers

Absolutely not. That's a big mistake many companies make. Women are very individual. When I talk about "women" I'm talking about a general guide. Not every woman is going to fit in the same slot, because we are all different. But we also share certain commonalities. It takes marketers, consultants, and coaches who thoroughly understand this to put together successful programs that will reach and impact the diversity of women in our country. Women consumers are stay-at-home moms, corporate executives, business owners, waitresses, doctors, and teachers. Even though there is diversity, women consumers share enough of the same characteristics, traits, and buying patterns to make it worthwhile to take notice of them.

The differences between Millennium, Gen X, Gen Y, and Baby Boomer women are tremendous. Those in the younger generations internalize their experiences through technology, wider shopping selections, higher expectations, and less brand loyalty than their parents. In the workforce, Millenniums, Gen Xs, and Gen Ys have seen people work for the same company for most of their careers, and then watched as retirement pensions and employment were sabotaged by fraud, greed, and criminal acts perpetrated by corporate executives.

Successful companies today must provide a new level of trust and integrity. They need to adapt their hiring and advancement policies to better fit the "instant gratification" mode of today's younger employees. These employees, both women and men, want to see diversity in upper management and feel they can rise within the organization. Companies need to help employees they want to retain develop a career path for now and the future that includes leadership training and support.

Wright

So what trends do you see for the future as far as marketing to women and women in leadership roles in organizations?

Myers

The Baby Boomer generation produced the brightest, best educated, most ambitious, and wealthiest women this country has ever had. Today, more women graduate college and are getting master's degrees than men. I see higher education continuing as a means for women's advancement. There will be more women in the pipeline who are qualified for C-suite positions and corporate board seats. Companies that want to keep talented women are going to have to groom them for upper management.

We have witnessed the first woman make a serious run for president. Women have become CEOs of Fortune 500 companies. Women business owners have created multi-million-dollar companies. Women are too talented and have too much financial power (remember, they spend eighty-five cents of every dollar) to not be sincerely sought after as consumers and executives.

Women's sports have become more mainstream with both genders watching women's golf and tennis events. But there is still a long way to go. Women are breaking barriers in golf, racing, sailing, and numerous other sports, and will continue to set records and excel in all areas of their lives.

Young women have a much more "can do" attitude because they haven't faced many of the hurdles their mothers and grandmothers confronted. Many of the changes in the younger population don't exist only in women. Gen X and Gen Y men have a different work ethic that corporations will have to adjust to. They want flextime and more team approaches to sales. Car dealerships, real estate offices, and other businesses should create a different dynamic to appeal to today's youth or risk becoming extinct.

With all the vast improvements and optimism for the future, there is still much inequality in many arenas. The pay gap—top salary disparity because of gender or race—and the number of women and minorities on corporate boards and in the C-suites are a few things that will begin to equalize in the next decade or two.

Wright

Well, what a great conversation! I had no idea that women had so much power and continue to exert their influence in shaping the future. I really appreciate the time you've taken to answer these questions. I certainly learned a lot.

Myers

I'm glad to provide as much information as possible to you because the more education people have in understanding the differences between men and women, the better for everyone. However, I always want to make sure that people know I am not in any way suggesting men are wrong or not doing things right—we're just different, and different makes life more interesting. Men and women are unique individuals and we should embrace and appreciate our dissimilarities. We each have our own thought processes and way of doing things. The more we understand about each other, the better it is for everyone.

Wright

Today we've been talking with Gerry Myers. She is CEO of Advisory Link. She is an international speaker, trainer, and consultant. Gerry is a pioneer in the women's market and the first author to publish a book on the topic, which is titled *Targeting the New Professional Woman: How to Market and Sell to Today's 57 Million Working Women*.

Gerry, thank you so much for being with us today on *Leading the Way to Success*.

About the Author

As CEO and President of Advisory Link, Gerry Myers helps corporations increase communications, marketing, and sales to women, as well as recruit, retain, and promote women within their organizations.

Myers, a pioneer in the women's market, is considered an expert on women. She is instrumental in creating awareness, training programs, keynote speeches, and consulting services for national and international companies, including many in the automotive and financial arenas.

With Myers at the helm, Advisory Link has formed numerous Women's Advisory Boards (WABs) across the country for many companies including MassMutual Financial Group, New York Life Insurance Company, and ClubCorp. She co-chaired ClubCorp's Women's Advisory Board on Organization Alliances and developed local WABs for New York Life in six cities and 14 WABs for MassMutual Financial Group. Additionally, she facilitates the Automotive Women Dealers, the Women's Initiatives in Corporations, and the Women Executives and Business Owners Exec-U-Links, which are peer coaching groups comprised of high-level executive women and business owners.

In addition to authoring *Targeting the New Professional Woman*, Myers has written articles and been featured or quoted as an authority on women in publications such as *The New York Times*, *American Demographics*, *WorkingWoman.com*, *Broker World*, *Independent Agent*, *The Financial Post*, *The Dallas Business Journal*, *Honolulu Weekly*, *Toronto Star*, *Marketing News*, *Dealer Magazine*, *MarketingProfs.com*, *Detroit Free Press*, *Christian Science Monitor*, *Brand Week*, and *Automotive News*. She has been a guest on a variety of radio and television talk shows.

She has been nominated for and has won numerous awards including the North Texas Commission's Entrepreneur Award, two Stevie Awards, and Women Business Council-Southwest Award.

Myers holds a Bachelor of Science degree from the University of Texas at Austin and a Master of Business Administration from the University of North Texas.

Gerry Myers
1408 Melody Breeze Ct.
Roanoke, Texas, 76262
817.379.0956
gerry@advisorylink-dfw.com
www.advisorylink-dfw.com

Gerry Myers

Chapter 10

Marilyn Tabor

THE INTERVIEW

David Wright (Wright)

Today we're talking with Marilyn Tabor. Marilyn is a national consultant and professional leadership coach. Since she began coaching in 1984, she has coached hundreds of leaders in a variety of leadership roles. She founded Organizational Dynamics Associates in 1995, and has become known for her expertise in highly diverse approaches to individual, team, group, and organizational coaching. She has designed a coaching process titled *Coaching for Excellence®*, and has authored a number of training programs created specifically for those interested in being influential leaders. Marilyn has a twenty-seven-year background in education that ranges from teaching to administration to professional development. Her consulting experience with individuals, school districts, non-profit organizations, and private-sector companies enables her to relate to the challenges facing today's leaders, and influences the practical perspective she brings to her work.

Marilyn, welcome to *Leading the Way to Success.*

Marilyn Tabor (Tabor)

Thank you, David. I'm honored to be included in this book project.

Wright

This book is about leading the way to success. Obviously, success holds different meanings for different people. So how do you define success?

Tabor

We often hear success defined as the achievement of a goal we've set or the positive conclusion of a plan or project. Sometimes success is described as hitting the target, doing what we set out to do, or even accomplishing something the way we wanted to do it. These can be substantial indicators of success, but I believe that *authentic success* always has an internal dimension to it. That dimension is an inner feeling of personal fulfillment that solidly connects the results we achieve to what matters to us and to the heart. I've come to understand that even when people meet or surpass every goal they set, without a vividly felt sense of personal fulfillment the resulting success seems incomplete or empty.

While the world may judge something we do as successful, *for us to consider something a true success requires that strong personal connection*. Let me share an example with you. Sarah is an educational administrator I've coached. She had achieved every goal she set and all the targets expected by the school district where she works. She chose to engage in a coaching relationship with me because she felt she was missing a sense of accomplishment as a professional, even though she was considered highly successful by those in top management and by her staff as well.

Not surprisingly, Sarah discovered that nearly all her success indicators were external. It seemed as if they didn't actually belong to her. It wasn't that she didn't think the goals and measures of success she had chosen were important. On the contrary, she did. However, she revealed that there was no sense of fulfillment for her—an absence of joy within as she viewed her so-called success. Whatever was needed for her to connect deeply to her work was missing for Sarah.

After a few sessions of coaching, Sarah discovered what mattered to her and touched her heart, the personal connection that created meaning for her. When she incorporated that connection within her goals, she experienced the result she had been looking for—a *feeling* of success!

For those leaders who may be concerned that effort will be diminished in some way if people seek an inner connection, there's an important truth to recognize. When we study successes that have been strongly connected to personal meaning and heart, we usually find *more* investment of energy and effort has been made, *not* less. So, my definition for true success includes the belief that success must be owned by and felt by the person, group, or organization that achieves it. And as leaders, we must find ways to make that happen for the people we lead as well as for ourselves.

Wright

So you believe there's a strong connection between leadership and the success of others. Just as success has many different meanings, so does the term "leadership." How would you define it?

Tabor

You're right, David. I do believe that leadership has a strong and vivid connection to the success of others; but the real meaning of leadership is extremely complicated to define. There are over 900 million entries on Google for leadership alone! I'm sure some of us think of leadership as a title or a role or even a position someone holds. The dictionary defines it as guiding others in a certain direction toward a result or conclusion. There are also many well-respected authorities on leadership whose work helps clarify this intricate concept—Peter Drucker, Warren Bennis, James Kouzes, Stephen Covey, and Jim Collins to name a few. I'll go out on a limb and add my own perspective to the many interpretations of leadership. Quite simply, I believe that *leadership is a way of being that influences others*. In other words, at its basic essence, the true meaning of leadership is influence.

It's important that we understand what influence is in the context of leadership, and what it is not. Influence is the power to have an effect on others or to bring about results without using coercion. It goes beyond title or role. It can be exhibited by the person at the top of the organizational ladder and also by the receptionist who manages the flow of business in the front office. When influence is paired with integrity, as it must be, a leader is able to promote positive shifts in both the perceptions and performance of others. Influence is not, and never should be, having power over others or controlling them. It's certainly not about manipulating people to achieve self-serving outcomes.

I discovered the power of influence by accident when I began coaching nearly twenty-five years ago and witnessed the powerful effects of deep listening, coupled with asking open-ended questions. I've also had the privilege of training, coaching, and consulting with many highly successful leaders who rely on influence to lead. Now this doesn't mean that influential leaders don't use authority when necessary; they do, and they do it skillfully. What I'm suggesting is that the leadership approach we choose most often, with most people, and in most situations, ought to be one of influence rather than control. Put simply, for me leadership equals influence, influence, influence!

Wright

You mentioned that you began coaching nearly twenty-five years ago. What insights have you gained during your experience as a coach that have shaped your approach to leading people to success?

Tabor

There are quite a few. When I first began coaching, the full responsibility of formal leadership wasn't a factor for me. As a new coach, I had the advantage of starting out by coaching students and colleagues, and occasionally coaching as an "informal" leader. It was so tempting to be "gently directive" during my early coaching days. As I gained experience, however, I found that the more directive I was during coaching, the more resistant people could be—sometimes subtly oppositional, occasionally becoming argumentative or even downright defensive. As a novice coach, I also found myself at times embedding my own ideas or advice into the conversation in the form of a question, which of course wasn't a question at all. As a coach, I don't do that anymore because I've learned that being directive rarely, if ever, leads people to success.

I also discovered that even when I was asked specifically for suggestions during coaching, those who asked didn't always try what I suggested. At first that was baffling to me. Over time, I understood that people are diligently searching to find answers. And when they can't find the answers within, they look outside themselves. The resulting problem, however, is that they have no ownership of those outside answers. That's a major reason why others tend not to act on the suggestions we make. Leading people to success calls for framing artful questions that will influence them to consider multiple options from which they can find answers, make personal choices, and move themselves forward to action.

As I continued developing my coaching skill, I became aware that I often worked harder at thinking and problem solving than the people I coached! It was frustrating because I knew it wasn't supposed to be that way. I finally learned to trust the most basic principle of coaching—the person being coached must do the mind work. As a result, I discovered that the more skillful I became as a coach, and the more I developed the art of masterful questioning, the more successful the people I coached were at finding their own answers, *and* taking responsibility for their own success.

As so many others have found, when I assumed my first formal leadership role, it was a learn-as-you-go experience. I did what I thought leaders were supposed to do—take charge, take action, be out in front, and lead the way. It took me some time to realize that the same things I had discovered during my development as a coach also applied to leadership.

The bottom line is that people are more likely to be successful when the ideas, the solutions, and the work come from them and belong to them. That insight led me to search for a way to take the best of what I knew and understood about coaching and combine it with the best of what I was learning and understanding about leadership. I call this blended approach "coaching-based leadership."

Wright

So as a leader, you found a unique approach called "coaching-based leadership." Will you say more about what makes coaching-based leadership different than other methods of leadership?

Tabor

Coaching-based leadership is a value-added approach that's coupled with the best leadership practices a person already utilizes as a leader. In this approach, leaders continue to make those choices and take those actions they are certain will lead to success, while at the same time, integrating two additional dynamic areas of focus into their daily leadership practice. One focus area is the genuine passion for developing people in ways that are good for both the individual and the organization. The other is the use of specific skill sets that are unique to the field of coaching and that are also known to influence others.

Regarding that first area of focus, I've found that most effective leaders feel passionately about developing the people whom they lead. The question is just how vigorously do we as leaders pursue this passion? There's so much that can get in the way—time, urgent demands, and the energy required to personalize this kind of development. To sustain this passion, we must believe that the return on the investment in developing people is so high that we cannot afford to neglect this as a major focus. For example, if pace is a factor in our success, by developing our people we can move forward more quickly. When quality is a criterion for success, developing people adds measurable value. If we want quality results, that level of result is far more likely to happen when we have invested energy in developing the people responsible for delivering those results. In effect, development of people becomes a purpose of its own, embedded within every goal set, every action planned and taken, and every interaction.

The second area of focus I mentioned is the use of specific skill sets that are drawn from the field of coaching and known to influence others. As I said earlier, I was a coach who had become a leader. I had learned the value of coaching and its extraordinary potential for influence, so I was determined to coach in my leadership role. How frustrating that goal became! There were so many people, and it was impossible to coach them all, one by one by one. At the same time, there was a tremendous need to influence groups of people when they worked in teams and in other large groups. It became imperative to figure out how to put leadership and coaching together in some way that would be both highly effective and time-efficient.

When we think of coaching in its more traditional form, we tend to envision one-to-one conversations where the person being coached chooses the direction and sets the agenda. While one-to-one conversations will always be an important format for leaders, so much of our leadership work occurs in group settings. Additionally, one of the most influential aspects of leadership is setting the vision and determining the direction for the organization and for those we lead.

So I chose to weave the six most powerful skill sets I had learned as a coach into my daily leadership practice. In that way, *coaching as a leader became about using the coaching skill sets, not about being a traditional coach*. The skill sets I selected were: 1) pausing for thought—what I call "mind work," 2) setting aside bias (i.e., being non-judgmental), 3) listening for focal points, 4) summarizing understanding, 5) asking inquiry questions, and 6) using varied and unique types of data or concrete evidence to influence direction.

Wright

Beyond the skills you identified, are there any particular values and beliefs that frame this coaching-based approach to leadership?

Tabor

Yes, there are, and they are the heart and soul of this leadership approach. The underlying values echo what many successful leaders would tell you are their values. For me, there are three that stand out and are fundamental to this type of leadership.

The first is integrity, demonstrated in the form of authenticity, honesty, and congruence. The reality is that people *allow* us to lead and be influential when we're authentic and display transparency. I'm talking about being true to ourselves, and showing our true selves—telling the truth, walking our talk, and talking our walk with consistency.

Another fundamental value is what I call respectfulness. It's making the very intentional choice to consider others and act in ways that reflect deep appreciation and compassion for humanity. Some may refer to this as establishing trust. However, I've found that having others trust me is sometimes beyond my control because of many factors having nothing to do with me. On the other hand, I *am* in control of my choice to be *trustworthy* and to act respectfully to others, showing courtesy and regard for them as human beings.

A third value crucial to a coaching-based approach is creativity. By that I mean the inventiveness, imagination, and willingness it takes to construct new ideas, new solutions, and new approaches. Creativity is at the heart of progress and forward movement. Einstein said it well, "Insanity is to keep doing the same things and expect different results." Tapping into creativity requires "lifting our own lids" to "go beyond the boxes" we find ourselves in that have been formed by habit, assumption, and perceived limitations. How fortunate we are to be in charge of lifting our own lids to find diverse ways of bringing about the results we want!

There are also four key beliefs that I think form the foundation for coaching-based leadership. First is the belief that true leadership is a continuous quest for excellence. As leaders, we set the example, discuss, model, support, and expect that quest of ourselves and from all those we lead in ways that give attention to mind, heart, and spirit. This type of attention is demonstrated by remembering that we are people first, and our work or roles second. This doesn't mean that we lower our standards for performance; rather, it means that we as leaders *focus on high performance as we both honor and respect people*. By doing so, the quest for excellence becomes personalized, creating that vivid connection I referred to earlier as being so necessary for success.

Another key belief is that the achievement of excellence or success is an inside-out process, meaning that excellence and success are constructed within. This construction is then demonstrated through our words, actions, and performance. Without that internal construction, the power of ownership and sustainability is missing. It's up to us as leaders to shape both the input and influence we provide others from which they construct their success, as well as the processes they use for that construction.

A third belief relates to the type of work culture needed to support and sustain success. Success is actually accelerated in a culture where threat is low and challenge is high, and where people engage in work and interactions that promote positive personal connections. If the threat is too high, the result is anxiety, and if challenge is too low, the result is apathy. It's maintaining a consistent balance between low threat and high challenge that leads to maximum capacity building and successful performance.

A final belief central to coaching-based leadership is one that reflects the importance of our commitment as leaders to developing self-directedness in ourselves and in those we lead. Simply put, self-directedness is a combination of self-confidence, mindful action, and resilience—essential elements of success. Influencing individual and group self-directedness becomes an ultimate goal in coaching-based leadership, one that builds the personal and organizational capacity necessary to support sustainable excellence.

Wright

You said the ultimate goal of coaching-based leadership is influencing the development of self-directedness. So what is self-directedness, and why do you believe that it leads the way to success?

Tabor

Self-directedness consists of the intentional and consistent practice of four interrelated capabilities, all of which are necessary for both high-level mind work and high-level performance.

The first capability is self-awareness. That means knowing our strengths and weaknesses, and noticing what's going on inside us. It is also the ability to observe ourselves in action, standing apart figuratively and noticing what we're saying or doing, as well as noticing the results we're getting and how others respond to us.

Self-management is the second capability linked to self-directedness. Basically, it means taking responsibility for ourselves. It requires having an inner sense of control over our own thoughts and emotions, our attitudes and habits, our perspectives and actions. It's being confident in the ability to problem-solve and produce results, and it requires having the resilience to bounce back when things don't go well. Self-management is a very necessary companion to self-awareness. After all, what difference would it make if we were highly aware of a particular behavior and didn't choose to do anything about it when it's not serving us well?

The third component of self-directedness is self-assessment, or the capability to monitor our own progress toward an intended outcome or goal. This means keeping track of how we're doing, checking in, and asking ourselves questions along the way: Are we meeting the outcomes that we've set? Are our personal standards being maintained? Are we making appropriate and timely progress? Self-assessment is also about using evidence to evaluate our own performance so that we are able to say upon reflection, "That was great!" or "Uh oh . . . not so great!" and know the reasons that make it so.

The final capability essential to self-directedness is self-improvement. That reflects a commitment to and a consistent striving for ongoing improvement. When we embrace self-improvement, we have an attitude that says, "As long as I'm on this earth, I'm a work in progress." Self-improvement also implies that we learn from our mistakes rather than repeating them. It signifies that we value flexibility and choose continuously to adapt and modify ourselves to respond to in-the-moment realities and to be the best we can be.

It's critical for leaders to understand that there is a direct relationship between self-directedness and success. Because self-directedness is affected by outside forces—not only by our feelings, thoughts, and needs— leaders can have a tremendous influence on the advancement of these capabilities in others. When the development of self-directedness is a high-priority leadership goal, consistently blended with other organizational, group, and individual goals, a leader is able to have a powerful impact on the growth of an extraordinary work force. That work force will practice high-level mind work as a norm, making the personal connections necessary to demonstrate initiative, responsibility, resourcefulness, and accountability—in other words, success!

Wright

You've used the intriguing term "mind work." Would you describe what mind work is and how is it connected to success?

Tabor

"Mind work" is the term I use to describe what we do when we engage, expand, or modify in some way both the reasoning and emotional processes that take place in the brain. I prefer "mind work" to the word "thinking" because what I'm referring to goes beyond logic and reasoning to include emotion, attitude, and even intuition. In applying coaching-based leadership, leaders intentionally engage and influence the mind work of the people they lead in order to promote success.

There are four different types of mind work, all of which have a tremendous impact on individual, team, group, and organizational success. The first type I identify as attitudinal mind work, engaging the mind around our likes and dislikes or our tendencies toward certain ways of being. Some examples include: Are we optimistic or pessimistic? Are we accepting or critical? Are we flexible or inflexible? Our attitudes can become fixed if they are not explored to determine their usefulness. So leaders need to be able to influence shifts in attitudes that don't contribute to success.

A second type is emotional mind work. There's a partnership in the brain between our emotional and thinking systems. This partnership instantly produces an emotional first impression of *everything* we experience. *Anything emotional receives preferential attention in the brain.* Strong emotion bypasses reasoning every time, whether we want it to or not. When leaders are skillful at acknowledging emotion—their own, as well as the emotions of others—and then influencing the mind work it takes to move beyond it, intense emotion need not become a barrier to success.

The third and most commonly known type is intellectual mind work. That's engaging in what we typically label as thinking—processes like planning, analysis, logic, and so on. I believe this kind of mind work tends to be work-culture-dependent, requiring a low threat, high challenge work culture to support the risk-taking necessary for the best, most creative thinking to take place.

The fourth type of mind work is probably the one we consider least often—intuitive mind work. This type of mind work is practiced by checking in with, paying attention to, and truly valuing the inner knowing or sensing that we all have, but that isn't dependent upon typical thought processes. This occurs at those times when we say, "I just know—" or "Something tells me—" or "My gut instinct says—." This type of mind work can sometimes be even more valuable than any other in terms of producing success. It is worthwhile for leaders to consider modeling and encouraging intuitive mind work as a common practice on the journey to success.

Wright

There are hundreds, perhaps thousands of books suggesting the skills leaders should have to be highly effective. What are the most significant skill sets that you think a leader must apply to influence the success of others?

Tabor

I have a definite bias, David! I mentioned earlier the six most powerful coaching skill sets that I believe can be woven into our daily leadership practice. From that list of six, I would give priority to listening for focal points, summarizing our understanding, and asking inquiry questions.

How I wish I had known the power of listening years ago! I'm referring to listening like a coach for the focal points embedded in people's communication that help us detect the meaning they are trying to convey. I'm absolutely convinced it's the single most valuable tool a leader has to determine the direction for influencing others. People communicate to us everything we need to know to make choices and decisions about in-the-moment influence, if we only listen.

Listening, however, is only half of a matched pair. Like salt and pepper, left and right, or up and down, listening is incomplete without summarizing our understanding. An *authentic* summary of what we hear communicated encompasses the *meaning;* it is not merely a reiteration of the words being spoken. When we summarize our understanding of the meaning, it indicates that we truly hear the message.

The results of skillful listening and summarizing can be extraordinary. Let me give you an example. I've had the privilege of working with one particular organization for four years now, providing leadership training and small-group leadership coaching for nearly seventy administrators and managers in a district of twenty-five schools. During that time, Ramon has advanced from principal, to director, to assistant superintendent. He believes that his coaching-based leadership approach has enabled him to be a more influential leader. His personalized version of it is to listen, hear and summarize the needs being expressed, remind himself not to do the mind work for others, and then influence them to discover their own answers and resolve their own problems.

Ramon recently described a labor negotiation where he was a member of the management team. Although both sides were near a settlement, they just couldn't quite get there. He focused on listening and summarizing. Over and over again, he summarized the feelings and needs being communicated by the other team. By summarizing and restructuring the wording of what was being communicated *without changing the basic meaning*, Ramon was able to facilitate a mutually beneficial settlement in record time. The lead negotiator for the other team commended him, saying, "Thank you for hearing what we were trying to say." To Ramon's pleased surprise, he was also elected by the other team as the facilitator for future negotiations because, as they said, "You know how to be impartial."

Another skill set I believe a leader must have in order to develop the success of others is that of asking influential inquiry questions. These are not ordinary questions. On the contrary, a powerful inquiry question launches a search for answers; and the real value lies in the search. Effective coaches and leaders are masterful at asking questions like that—open-ended questions that support people in working out solutions on their own, rather than telling them what to do or persuading them to do things in a certain way.

On an interesting side note, science is helping us understand why inquiry-type questions have such power. Apparently, when people search for answers and solve the problem themselves, the brain releases a rush of neurotransmitters that cause alertness, prepare the body for action, and pave the way for insights to be discovered.

In their work related to the neuroscience of leadership, David Rock and Jeffrey Schwartz describe findings based on MRI and EEG technologies suggesting that at a moment of insight, a very complex set of new connections is actually created in the brain. These connections have the potential to enhance mental resources and overcome our natural resistance to change! So one way to influence success is by asking inquiry questions that both generate and deepen moments of insight.

Wright

How could someone who is reading this interview and is interested in this coaching-based approach to leadership put some of these ideas into action tomorrow?

Tabor

Starting tomorrow is simple! By the way, David, we've been talking about this coaching-based approach in the context of leadership. The truth is that *this is a highly effective approach for all communication*—whether we are interacting with family, friends, co-workers, or those for whom we have leadership responsibility.

Anyone can begin by merely choosing to listen in a more attentive and deeper way. All that is required is a willingness to believe that listening actually can produce the same kind of results that Ramon experienced. Choosing to listen also necessitates the self-management to set aside the distractions of the mind that we all experience, and to slow down long enough to truly listen for understanding. Quite simply put, if you want to experience the influence that can result from a coaching-based approach to any communication, just listen more and listen better.

Another way to start tomorrow is to begin asking open-ended questions that promote mind work. Of course we have great advice to offer, and we're good problem-solvers. That's probably how we became leaders in the first place. Advice giving and doing the mind work for others can be quite seductive, and it often seems a quicker, more direct path to get the results we want. Unfortunately, both giving advice and doing the mind work that others need to do for themselves undermine the profound influence that we can have through inquiry.

To develop the skill of inquiry, we have to believe in the capacity of others and in their positive intentions. It also requires that we place a much higher value on developing others to do their own vision creating, goal setting, action planning, problem solving, and choice making, rather than the value we place on doing it for them. By the way, it will be helpful to remember that listening and inquiry take practice, practice, and more practice to reach the level of proficiency that we all prefer to have.

Wright

You've shared a wide variety of ideas during this interview. What memory bytes would you like people to take away and hold onto after reading this chapter?

Tabor

Perhaps what would be most valuable for any reader to remember, whether or not he or she has a vested interest in leadership, is the indisputable connection between mind work and success. Each of us is in charge of our own mind work, and is highly capable of developing all four types to support our own success. Engaging and respecting attitudinal, emotional, intellectual, and intuitive mind work leads the way to inspired options and unlimited possibilities for achieving success.

I'd also like people to remember that coaching-based leadership (or coaching-based communication) is an intentional choice. It's a choice that supports both important and sustainable progress, and increases a leader's ability to have significant influence on individual, team, group, and organizational success. I believe the strength of coaching-based leadership lies within the unity of two powerful forces—the best of leadership and the best of coaching. That combination influences success through the mind, the heart, and the spirit.

Wright

What a great conversation! I appreciate the time you've taken to answer all these questions for me today. I have really learned a lot, and you've given me a lot to think about.

Tabor

I'm glad you found something of value to consider! I've appreciated this opportunity, David, and it was a sincere pleasure talking with you.

Wright

Today we've been talking with Marilyn Tabor, a national consultant and leadership coach. Her work, and that of her consulting associates, is dedicated to influencing exceptional performance and professional excellence by building personal, team, group, and organizational capacity in three major areas: influential leadership practices, building collaborative work cultures, and guiding systemic change. One of Marilyn's several areas of focus is group leadership coaching. In various school districts where this has become a part of the work culture, she and her associates create a shared leadership development experience and coach teams and job-alike groups of administrators and managers regarding their greatest leadership challenges.

Marilyn, thank you so much for being with us today on *Leading the Way to Success*.

About the Author

Marilyn Tabor, a consultant and leadership coach, has coached over a thousand people in various roles since she began in 1984. After founding Organizational Dynamics Associates in 1995, she has earned a reputation for her unique approaches to individual, team, group, and organizational coaching. She is the originator of *Coaching for Excellence®,* and has authored a number of training programs designed for those who want to increase their influence as leaders. With her twenty-seven-year background in education that includes teaching, administration, and professional development, Marilyn is a skilled group facilitator and engaging keynote speaker. Her experience with individuals, school districts, non-profit organizations, and public companies has honed her understanding of the complexity facing today's leaders, and shaped the practical perspective she offers audiences and clients. Her work is dedicated to influencing exceptional performance and professional excellence by growing personal, team, group, and organizational capacity in three areas: influential leadership, building a collaborative culture, and guiding systemic change. She has recently introduced an approach that has the potential to transform interactions in the workplace by viewing all business relationships as if each were with a "customer." This approach centers on creating, developing, and sustaining relationships as the foundation for success.

Marilyn Tabor
Organizational Dynamics Associates, Inc.
23531 Lochlomond
Laguna Niguel, CA 92677
949.452.4011
odaTabor@cox.net
www.coachforexcellence.com

Chapter 11

Valarie Willis

Valarie Willis (Willis)

In the halls of companies across the states, one hears the reverberation of "do more with less." The notorious downsizing, where one can still hear the screech of the tape gun, as boxes are filled with personal belongings that no longer have a corporate or factory home, moves across many industries. No place is safe from the painful slicing of downsizing, not hospitals, automotive, government, private sector or non-profits.

Those who have temporarily escaped the swath of the downsizing hatchet are left to pick up the pieces, add to their workload, meet new deadlines and, oh yes, by the way, serve the customer and create compelling experiences.

Many a CEO and others have paced the floors in offices and boardrooms wondering how to still meet the goals and objectives, and how to motivate the employees that are left and for some, how to motivate themselves.

Downsizing is deflating the attitudes of many workers, like a tire with a slow leak. At some point in time, the people stop caring, feeling that the leadership has stop caring about them. They often develop a "wait and see" attitude or many start the retirement countdown clock that loudly ticks their time away. It is so bad, that many can tell you down to the minute, how long they have until they leave. The people come to work, hunker down, do their jobs and go home with little passion or energy about the job. This is a dangerous concoction for companies today.

I have experienced first hand what it is like to be left in the aftermath of a downsizing tsunami. Neither will leave you filled with joy and excitement to return to work, and performance can suffer greatly.

While the leader may not have had a choice in the downsizing decision, the leader has a choice in how they will respond and how they will care for those left behind. The role of the leader is to connect with their employees and create an environment where the employees will be successful and can bring all their talents into play.

David Wright (Wright)

How should leaders respond in the aftermath of a downsizing?

Willis

How a leader responds and behaves within the next twenty-four hours following a downsizing can make a critical difference. Jeff was the director of an IT group for a major manufacturing company in the mid-west that had experienced a major downsizing, actually more than once. At the end of what would become known as "Black Friday", Jeff pulls his team together to talk about the day and what happened.   Jeff took the time to listen to the concerns of those who remained, he made no false promises about the workload that was left behind, but instead vowed to work with everyone to strategize how to operate together. Jeff spent considerable time in the following days having one on one meeting with the team, encouraging them, being understanding about the relationships that were impacted. He understood that losing long time colleagues was like a painful divorce and people needed to able to express themselves. Jeff took the time to show care and concern for each team member, finding out what they needed to move forward and he stayed visible, while other leaders took refuge in their offices, hoping that the questions would go away.

Jeff's team excelled despite the challenges, because his team knew that they were cared for, his team willingly went the extra mile, stayed the extra hours, and gave up discretionary time during a very difficult transition. People working on Jeff's team would tell you that Jeff cared about them, their work and their personal success. In return for his dedication to them, they worked steadfast to achieve the goals.

Whenever there are major situations in the workplace, whether it is downsizing or major changes, a leader needs to remain visible and the leader's voice needs to be heard frequently with consistent messages. As one leader said to me, "a leader must over communicate to reach everyone and to create an open environment where people feel safe to speak their mind." Messages that inspire the employees refocus their efforts and affirm the positive actions that are being taken.

Events that brings the staff together to discuss vision, strategies, current realities and the road ahead will help associates bring their voice to the situation and allows the leaders to quiet the rumor mill before it grows too rapidly.

It should not take a major catastrophe for leaders to pay attention to their employees. Before downsizing and major changes, leaders should create trust and credibility so that they can keep employees engaged in the down turns. One may be wondering if that is possible and be assured that it is.

Wright

How do you create an environment that is caring for employees?

Willis

Care is the new four letter word that companies need to start embracing. Those companies that can authentically demonstrate care for their employees will be greatly rewarded, often in unexpected ways.

American Micro is a precision machining company in Batavia, Ohio, they have discovered the secret to having increased sales in a down market. American Micro has experience fifteen percent increases, while other similar companies are down or out of business. A part of their secret is that little four letter word called CARE. In an interview with Haze H. Flowers, Director of Human Resources for American Micro, he shares that in their organization, taking care of the talent is a top priority. American Micro ensures that everyone in the organization from the janitor to the CEO, Pierre Paroz has a development plan. To be sure that their company has the necessary skills for the future, American Micro has developed their own vocational school and employees are constantly learning new skills and developing their talents. The associates here feel valued and appreciated.

American Micro creates an open and caring environment by having multiple communication strategies in the works. They hold quarterly town hall meeting, monthly Leadership Luncheon (or breakfast) for every shift in the organization and all the executives spend time on the factory floor talking with the employees. The employees get to share what is working well and where their pain points are. The leaders take these conversations to heart and many process improvements have come as a result of these open sessions. The people feel comfortable to speak freely because they know their opinions count and that they are valued. As Tom Peters says, "all the answers to the problems in organizations can be solved by front line workers, if we would only bother to ask them."

The employees find ways to regularly celebrate accomplishments and the newsletter that the employee produce, gives everyone an opportunity to share any reason that they have to be celebrated or acknowledged.

Caring does not stop with building employee relationships and open communication, the company has taken another big step. They have recently implemented an initiative that helps employee achieve both professional and personal goals. When you focus on the employees and what they care about, in return productivity is higher, absenteeism is reduced, efficiencies increases and there is an overall higher level of employee engagement and retention.

Flowers said, "When people are engaged,(and they will be when they feel cared for), then they will own the process, there are fewer distractions, they are more productive and efficient, In return, we have happier customers, achieve the business goals and it is a win-win for everyone." When you care for your employees, you can reduce turnover in the organization. When you have high turnover that is the equivalent of entrusting your company to a group of strangers.

Caring does make a different, intrinsically and to the bottom line.

Wright

In what sense do you use the word care?

Willis

The word care can be used in many different ways, it is most often thought of in the sense of attending to the needs (often personal) of others. We think about how we have to care for our aging population. Soldiers that receive packages, known as "care packages" when they are serving away from home, view these packages as an act of thoughtful acknowledgement of their work. The word care is about the "power of care", the little small acts of attention and kindness that leaders can do to support, uplift and engage their employees. Leaders that understand the power of daily recognizing and acknowledging their employees will have an advantage with their employees during the tough times. Employees are more likely to stick it out, stay around and be engaged when they know that their leader cares for them.

Care can be thought of as 'touchy feely', however, small acts of attentiveness, addressing people by their name, giving direct eye contact, and truly listening to people are the acts of care that can transform relationships.

Others have described care as being considerate, aware, attentive, focused on positive, made to feel important, being sensitivity, being held in high regard and respected. There are a lot of opportunities for leaders to care and it does not take a lot out of one's schedule to show appreciation and concern for others. Care is more than "touchy feely", leaders expect their workers to show up, they have to realize that people bring their heart as well as their minds to the job.

Many leaders shy away from being caring leaders because they may not be ready to address what people may tell them and it does open up to the possibility of becoming vulnerable. Vulnerability is part of being an authentic leader.

Wright

The word "care" is often viewed as touchy/feely, how do we get over that?

Willis

Start by looking the word up in the dictionary and the definitions will surprise you. Care is defined as, "a state of mind in which one is troubled;

Valarie Willis

worry, anxiety, or concern: He was never free from care. 2. a cause or object of worry, anxiety, concern, etc.: Their son has always been a great care to them. 3. serious attention; solicitude; heed; caution: She devotes great care to her work. Lastly, to be concerned or solicitous; have thought or regard.

If leaders were to pay "serious attention, have a state of mind where they concerned themselves about their employees, of view their employees of being worthy of concern and high regard, anxiety and worry, these are not 'soft' issues, they are ones of great concern. We get over the bias of care being touchy/ feely, as we come to understand that care is at the core of successful organizations. Just as the exercise of pilates strengthens the core muscles so that everything else on the body works well together, care is the core of relationships and the core of great cultures and is at the core of successful leaders.

Some of the best companies in the industries have caring cultures, think about Southwest Airlines which go out of their way to take care of the well-being of their employees and find creative ways to celebrate. At Southwest Airlines, Herb Kelleher, former CEO said, "We have always felt that a company is much stronger if it is bound by love rather than by fear." The statement defines the company's leadership philosophy. The company calls its employees their first customer; the main function of leadership is to serve employees. To do that a leader has to be dedicated to others, not to the burnishing of his or her ego." Here is a company who values their employees and cares deeply for them, even loves them.   When an employee experiences a catastrophe or tragedy, the people of Southwest band together to help the employee, whether that means sending help, packing up items from a flood or giving financial support, they will be there.

In the retail industry where employee turn-over is usually high, one mass retailer has found a way to retain their employees. Jim Sinegal is CEO of Costco, the 5th largest retailer and his philosophy is, "if you take care of your employees, they will take care of the business." Sinegal pays his employees above average wages and believes that his employees should be able to afford the American dream of owning a home. Costco has figured out a way to balance caring for the people and managing the business. Although Wall Street has accused Sinegal of being too benevolent towards his employees, Senegal understand both the business benefits and the intangible benefits of caring for his workforce. Looking at the stock value of Costco and how they have out performed others in their market, Sinegals' leadership philosophy is working well.

Wright

How do employees want to be motivated or cared for?

Willis

Leaders face the challenge of motivating their staff on a daily basis. The study done by Gallup in 2003 indicates that 59% of the people in the U.S. come to work in a disengaged state of mind. They show up, suck up the air, expend little energy and could care less about their job and often those around them.

Leaders are under a mis-conception about motivation. Leaders really cannot motivate someone else, instead they are charged with creating the environment. Leaders believe that they need to become the daily cheerleader, or drill captain or come up with elaborate schemes to get their employees motivated. Don't misunderstand, leaders should be cheerleaders and visible, but all the fanfare done in an insincere manner, done without genuinely caring about their team, is missing the point. When employees were asked what motivated them, the key responses were:

- To be listened to
- Being respected
- Receiving appreciation
- Sharing of information
- Challenging opportunities
- A show of concern
- A word of encouragement

These attributes could be summarized as the ability to care. Care, according to the dictionary, means to be concerned to, pay serious attention or to worry. Employees need their leaders to pay serious attention to what is needed to create the optimal workplace. Most people that responded to the question, "how do you stay motivated", indicated that they were self-motivated and only needed the leader to recognize and appreciate their performance and create an inspiring environment.

"One of the biggest complaints employees have is they are not sufficiently recognized their organizations for the work that they do," according to a study done by Knowledge and Wharton doctoral student, Ramarajan. (Knowledge.warton.upenn.edu) "When an employee does not think that the organization respects and values them, ,they tend to experience higher levels of burnout," said Ramarajan.

Wright

What are the experts saying?

Willis

According to a study put out by the Hay Group – only one-half of the people they interviewed felt that their companies cared about their well being. Interesting, because companies today are asking their employees to care about the customer, the patient or the client. So why shouldn't they as a leader care about the employee? Care is a cycle; when the leader shows care for the employee, the employees will show care for one another and then the employees can care for the customer, patient or or client. That results in higher levels of customer satisfaction. I call this the Care Connection. Let me give you an example.

At American Micro, the employees care for each other and rally around employees who are in need of help. When employee basic needs are met, they are more focused at the task in hand. According to Walker and Sorkin in a recent book published by Wiley and Sons, " people are driven to satisfy or protect their own basic psychological needs, including survival, belonging, power, fun and freedom. And satisfaction of these needs in the workplace is so important that if they are not met, many employees are quick to choose resignation over a a need injustice. " (Training Magazine July/August 2008)

Additionally, the people at American Micro regularly engage in activities that give back to the community to help others in need. They extend their caring model outside of the work environment.

As there are more Generation Y entering into the workforce, those 25 and under, it is important to understand that this generation grew up on praise and attention. Therefore when they come into the workforce, they will be expecting the same, feedback and praise. That will require leaders to be attentive and caring about their employees. (Sharon Birkman Fink – Birkman International)

How does one create compelling customer experiences if they feel uncared for? Caring people will care for others in spite of behaviors of their leaders, but more people could care and care deeper when they see that the leader cares. Why should an employee care about the company if they feel that the company doesn't care about them? Leaders should not be surprised by the levels of cynicism in the organization if they are not holding their employees in high regard, an act of caring.

In Business Week of November 2000, Joyce Fletcher, author *of Disappearing Acts: Gender, Power, and Relational Practice at Work* said, "Employees who feel cared about by their bosses or are inspired by them often produce higher-quality work." If an act of caring can produce higher quality work, why wouldn't every leader want to participate in caring

In a study performed by Reuter in April 2008, they found that the intrinsic motivation of "paying people a compliment, activates the same reward center in the brain as paying them cash." It seems that compliments given in a sincere manner is a powerful technique that uplifts employees.

Wright

What is the impact of care on the customer experience?

Willis

Creating Compelling Customer Experiences – Everywhere we turn, there are articles about the need for companies to create compelling customer experiences. In order to create compelling experiences, we need associates who care about the client, and the customers and if the leaders don't care about them, why should they care about the experience?

At a prominent manufacturing company, there was a senior executive who constantly berated people, and left them scathing voice mail messages at all hours of the night. When the customer service representatives would come in the next morning and check voice mails, these debilitating messages would be heard. It would be difficult for the customer service representative to be upbeat and positive and deliver excellent customer service in an environment that devalued an deflated them. It came as not surprise that the levels of customer service were in dire need of improvement.

Leaders have great influence in the organization and should take care that they do not abuse the power of influence.

In organizations that provide personal service, such as hospitals, nursing homes, assisted living centers, nail salons, spas, etc., the staff needs to be able to show care and compassion for the customer. How do they learn how to do this, where are the examples that show them what care looks like and feels like? Imagine that you work for a leader who doesn't acknowledge your presence, treats you like an assumption and doesn't speak to you as they pass by. Yet, in the town hall meetings, you hear this same leader talk about how as an organization they must care about the patient, customer or client and how they must create compelling interactions that the customer, patient or client will respond to. It is enough to leave you wondering what to believe and what to do.

The employee is not going to know how to respond to that message, as the employee doesn't see caring behaviors being acted out. At best, an employee may respond in a nonchalant manner in how they treat the customer, patient, or client, but being nonchalant, won't give someone a reason to return and become a loyal constituent.

Wright

What happens when leaders don't show that they care?

Willis

Meet Mary who has been described as efficient, cheerful, caring, serving, productive and a customer service person extraordinaire. When Mary retired, she decided to take a job working three days a week at a local dealership. She had heard great things about the dealership that her friend was employed by, and thought the job would be perfect. Armed with years of customer service experience, a winning attitude, Mary starts her new job as a receptionist for an up-scaled car dealership. Within days, Mary knew she had made a mistake. The dealership manager barely mumbled a hello upon arriving, and the culture was one where people feared the manager and the manager issued orders like a drill sergeant. People would be corrected publicly and nothing ever pleased him. The manager didn't want Mary greeting the customers as they entered, that was the sales person's job, even though Mary was the first person that they would see . Instead sales people would scramble to get to the door like un-choreographed dancers..

"How could this place be so different?, "Mary wondered, at the other location, her friend was happy, engaged and energized. The manager there was thoughtful, considerate, kind and caring. The dealerships may have been selling the same cars, but they weren't delivering the same level of internal experience.

One day, a major snow storm was approaching the city, the first dealership took into consideration their staff and the safety of the staff getting home, after all, most car buyers are not out shopping on a cold snowy day. At the dealership where Mary worked, they were required to stay until the normal closing time, although not a soul came in to buy a car Mary felt as if the needs and safety of the employees took a back seat to a "possible" snow day sale.

It was no surprise that Mary left this job, the other associates missed her smile and happy banter, but they all knew without asking why she left, she left for the same reason that the others had left, the manager didn't care about her or her well-being. Mary wasn't the first receptionist to leave, the job was like a revolving door, they came and went. To this day, the manager of that particular dealership doesn't know that his behavior is driving away people and even those that remain, can't be performing at optimal levels, coming into a caustic work environment.

In the same city a few miles away is another dealership that sells the exact same brand of cars and the associates there feel totally different about their experience. The leader in the other facility has been described as flexible, kind, considerate, and accommodating. The workers there feel that their is a reciprocal agreement and are willing to go the extra mile when needed. The turnover rate at this location is considerably lower, trust levels are considerably higher and the energy that one feels in the dealership is warm and friendly, as opposed to cool and sterile. The difference is the leader's ability to care.

"When leaders do not care, they miss the opportunity to get free advertising from engaged employees, they have performance and productivity gaps and they fall short on their ability to attract and retain the best employees," said Haze Flowers. In a manufacturing environment, when leaders don't care, it manifest itself in higher absenteeism, lower efficiencies, more litigation and higher worker comp claims.

Wright

What is the effective of positive leader behavior?

Willis

Kouzes and Posner, authors of The Leadership Challenge™ for years have talked about their research on the behaviors of leaders and that people watch the leader's behavior. In the example above the leader was not demonstrating the kind of behavior that should be repeated in the culture. The leaders behavior didn't match the brand promise of this particular dealership. Having a mis-alignment in leadership behavior and brand promise may impact the profitability of the company. People do not perform at their best in hostile environments, Mary knew that if she stayed, she would not be working at her optimal level, as the leader kept shutting her down.

Positive leadership behavior has a direct impact on the level of engagement and productivity in the workplace according to a study conducted by Greenberg and Arakawa in 2007, "the researchers found that employee optimism was related to employee engagement, which, in turn, was correlated with greater performance." Positive leadership includes the act of caring for those in the workplace.

Leaders who care sometimes have to take the initiative to change the environment that people are working in. Leaders cannot change people, however leaders can change or create positive caring cultures which, allow people to thrive.

Wright

How do you create a caring environment?

Willis

Alix Raine, SVP of Communications North America for United Business Media LLC, a leading global media company, did exactly that. She suspected that people weren't performing to their fullest, many were burned out, and levels of collaboration were low across the various business units. Her suspicions were confirmed based on a corporate communications survey indicating employee interest in collaboration among the different divisions of the company.

Alix knew that when people are busy, trying to get them away from their jobs is like pushing a boulder uphill. There had to be a way to bring people together, impart key information and create a sense of community where there was dysfunction. The concept of the Power Hour was born, Alix created an initiative where she brought together representatives from all the different business units from Boston to California and asked them for input and feedback as to what people needed. This team became "agents" who would create community building activities that would only last for an hour. The other key element was that the entire Power Hour had to be hosted by the agents, so that they would own the process and feel connected. Power Hour was created as a new information platform that would also involve and engage the employees.

Its objectives were:
1. to educate employees
2. to encourage collaboration companywide
3. to raise morale

The Power Hour fostered networking opportunities, showcased the company's products and services, provided current market trends and increased networking. It was a 60-minute quarterly face-to-face event hosted by "agent" employees at each branch.

The agents found ways to feature other employees through video and by highlighting their work. Key information was imparted through interviews, videoed skits and using game show formats. Power Hour was considered to be, "for the people, by the people." Each Power Hour event was planned by the 'agents', therefore there was buy-in and commitment. The results of these Power Hours which occurred every quarter were that people became more engaged, more collaborative and more informed. The agents changed on an annual basis, so they didn't burn out and new ideas were always flowing.

Those who attended the Power Hours found them to be invigorating and felt that their voice had been heard through the survey and that leadership cared about what they thought and who they were. A follow up survey confirmed these results:

"There is broad agreement among attendees that Power Hour gives employees "a broader perspective" about United Business Media - thus giving employees a unique channel for learning more about and keeping current with United Business Media LLC initiatives. Most attendees agree that the Power Hour allows them to meet, network and collaborate with other employees. Roughly three attendees in four also agree that Power Hour sessions are "fun to attend and participate in."

"Business is about people; and effective leaders recognize that people are their most important asset," said Alix Raine, Senior Vice President Communications North America, United Business Media, LLC. "When valued and encouraged to contribute, I believe you can count on employees to work together to exchange ideas and develop innovative solutions that advance shared business objectives.

Most leaders can find an hour in their busy schedules to connect to their employees and make a difference on a quarterly basis. Because Alix cared, she was willing to pursue this initiative against the tide and worked diligently to win people over and to show others that taking the time to care, make a difference and involve the employees can create success. Bringing people together, showcasing their skills and involving them in the process re-energized the employees.

Wright

Why should leaders care?

Willis

Employees who feel their leaders care and are concerned about their welfare are more likely to more committed, give up discretionary time and be more engaged. Leaders who care can create environments which are more conducive to positive behavior which, can impact the level of services and the experiences that both internal and external customers will receive. When employees know that leaders care and have done all they can to provide the best benefits and show appreciation, the employees can focus more on their jobs and less on other matters. The workers at Costco know that they are fairly paid, (higher than industry norm), that their health care is taken care of and recognition and appreciation is the order of the day, so they can relax and do their jobs well.

In the *Leadership Challenge*™ book, we find that, "genuine acts of caring uplift the spirits and draw people forward." We all know that when spirits are uplifted, people are apt to perform better, have happier attitudes and those attributes cascade into the work and how they treat others. The other critical component of an organization is the culture and the people that work there. People like working with other people who are positive and uplifting. Think about the number of birthday cakes and celebrations those organizations have, or other reasons to eat and get together. Why do we do these things? Because they uplift people's spirits, it shows others that we care about them and it creates a spirit of one community and brings people together.

In today's business world where we rely heavily on technology, there is still much to be said about bringing people together face to face. Organizational collaboration is essential in getting projects done in an efficient manner and an open manner. Collaboration happens when people can trust each other, which means that they have to know one another. One way to build trust is to genuinely care about the 'whole' person, not just the work that gets done. Care improves relationships and impacts the bottom line.

Wright

Can you share an example?

Willis

Cassandra has worked for both large and small organizations. In the interview she was asked to think about the leaders/supervisors that she reported to and what that relationship was like. When Cassandra spoke about at an organizational level, her remarks were not as positive about the larger organization, however when she thought about specific people, the views changed. The common denominators that Cassandra found in both of the leaders that she admired and remembered well, was their ability to be flexible, accommodating and that helped her career grow. As a result of her leader's ability to care, Cassandra was more flexible and accommodating in her relationship both with her supervisors and with others around her. She collaborated more with others to get things done and to juggle the schedules.

Wright

Can care impact an organization's brand?

Willis

Care is a cultural attribute, which can be imbedded in the brand. Given that culture is a reflection of leadership and behavior, if the leaders show the behavior of care, then one would expect to see that reflected in the culture, which becomes part of the brand. As baby boomers are aging and assisted living centers are becoming more prevalent, would one not expect to see and feel the act of caring within that culture. In the service industry, from fast food, to health care, people who genuinely care can greatly impact the levels of service in a positive way and therefore impact the brand. You know when someone does not care about their job or what they are doing. You can tell by how they treat you and how attentive they are to the details about the job. Just start observing the behaviors that you personally experience in your organization and rate them on a "Care Scale" of 1 to 10.   What do you see? Next rate your own behavior and see how well you do. Take a look at your observations and create an action plan to improve.

Leaders who feel that care needs to be a core value for their culture need to assess their culture and determine if the value of care is being lived out. Whether care becomes a core value or not, individual leaders can demonstrate care as a personal value.

In organizations where people experience care, it will be easier for them to care for the customer and create wonderful experiences for others. The retail industry is a prime example of how employee care directly manifests itself to the customer. The Container Store is known to treat their employees well, are concerned about their welfare and rigorously train their employees. They pay their employees at the top end of the industry and they will not hire anyone who does not fit the brand and culture. Container Store has discovered that being clear on their values and hiring those who espouse the values is far better than just 'filling an opening." Container Store has created a caring culture for both their employees and customers and have embedded this experience in all their transactions.

Wright

Can you teach someone to care?

Willis

Can you teach people to care has been asked on several occasions and coming to grips to an answer has not been easy. If you believe that care is skill, then one has to believe that care can be taught, just as leadership is a skill and can be taught. One has to want to care, just as one has to want to lead in order to learn how to care. Care can be learned by doing with positive reinforcement.

If we aren't able to teach care, the service industry will be in big trouble. As the baby boomers are aging and rehabilitation and health care services increase, those industries will need people who fundamentally understand the act of caring. Imagine going into a rehabilitation center or assisted living center and be served by those who do not care about your well being? Would you continue to go there, or place your loved ones into these facilities? Not likely. Leaders of these establishments are going to have to understand the essence of care, demonstrate the act of caring, and teach others to care. Care will have to become imbedded into the fabric of the organization. The absence of care will lead to lower levels of service, which will eventually have a negative effect on the bottom line.

Wright

Is there an example of a company that is trying to teach people to care?

Willis

The Make-A-Wish Foundation of Ohio/Indiana/Kentucky, a non-profit organization run by CEO & President Susan McConnell addressed the issue of teaching care. Susan discovered that her staff did a great job of taking care of their clients, but did not quite do an equally great job of creating an

```
Valarie Willis

internal caring environment. That gap created a  brand mis-alignment between what they represented  to the external world and how they represented themselves internally. Susan embarked on creating a culture of care by bringing her entire staff together at the  annual retreat and discussing the attributes of care and how each person on a daily basis could make a difference. People were allowed to define care and think about examples of care and then think about how they have demonstrated care.  The team created visual images that represented care, which became their reminder to behave in caring ways.   Each person attending randomly selected a "care partner", someone that throughout the upcoming year, they would be responsible for, in some small way.  Learning to care is active learning through small steps.  Each person left with a personal "Care Journal" to track their behaviors and Susan established a Care award, to reinforce the value of care.  As Susan Berger said, "When you care, people notice."  When leaders care, their employees notice, so leaders need to model the act of caring and then others can learn how to care through them.

Susan has created the "Spirit of Care" award to help reinforce the caring behaviors that are so important to her non-profit agency.

**Wright**

Where do leaders fail their constituents?

**Willis**

By not taking time to get to know them and to understand what is important to them and what they value.  Research by Barry Posner has proven that employees that are clear about their own personal values have a higher level of commitment to the organization.  Many time leaders don't find out what people value.  That should start in the interview process.  I learned that one of my leadership mistakes was not hiring the right person and as I look back on some of those hiring snafus, I realize that the people I hired innately had a different set of personal values than would work in the organization.   Care is a value, and if that value is important to your organization, then it should be tested for.  Find out how someone has acted in a caring manner, set up a scenario and find out how that person

186
```

would respond. Hiring the right people and then creating the right environment will lead to a caring culture.

Because everyone is so busy and times are so hectic, the last thing most leaders want to do is spend time taking someone to lunch or grabbing a cup of coffee, but that small gesture can pay a leader back in spades. How else do you discover what makes people tick and what they are passionate about? When you can match people's passion to the work, you have a winning formula. Giving time and attention to others is a great act of caring.

Meet Peter Brunelle, former Group President of a major shoe manufacturer , who was one of the most caring leaders in that company. Peter had a daunting travel schedule through the states and across the world; however, he always found time to connect with his staff. Peter regularly checked in on Monday mornings, no matter where he was, he always inquired as to what was going on with the staff, who had performed exceptional customer service and what needed to be acknowledged. When Peter would return to the office, he made it a point to stop by people cubicles and thank them for their extra effort. You could find Peter in the Board room or the warehouse, he made it his business to connect with the people who helped run his business.

Peter would best be described as a quiet unassuming individual who had the ability to transform organizations. Within two years, Peter had totally transformed a lethargic division into one that exceeded their plans.

Those leaders who only ask about the numbers of the day and fail to acknowledge the people that work for them are leading in the dark. Many organizations think that they are doing a good job in recognizing employees, yet when the employees are surveyed, there is a considerable gap in how recognition is being perceived. Employers are falling short in the recognition department and not yet figured out that recognition is as vital as wages and benefits. (Investors Business Daily, October 28, 1999).

Wright

What specifically should leaders do to show others that they care?

Willis

Ways to Create Caring Relationships

1. Write a personal note when someone does something noteworthy, either personally or professionally. In today's world of technology, personal notes are becoming rare, which makes them more valuable.
2. Create an update pipeline, a way to keep you connected and to know what is going on in the organization. You can't be everywhere, so get connected to those who can keep you informed.
3. Give someone 5-10 dedicated minutes of your time and presence. No phone interruptions, no blackberries, no pagers. Listen and be interested in what the person is saying. Summarize to show that you are listening, ask questions.
4. Find a way to show appreciation to people who are living the values, exceeding goals, living the brand and/or realizing the vision. Make recognition a part of your daily routine.
5. Remove an obstacle or pave a way to help someone in their career or project. Be attentive about people's ability and find a way to use their skills.
6. Ask people about their opinion on policies, changes, ways to accomplish the goal, listen and take notes. If you use an idea, be sure to give appropriate credit.
7. Find ways to show people that you care. Some random acts of care can create long tern employee loyalty.
8. Give positive feedback for exceptional work or taking a good risk. Celebrate those behaviors that are helping you move towards your goal.
9. Stay close to your best performers, take them to lunch and find out what they need to continue to be successful. Don't ever take your key performers for granted,
10. See the greatness in those that work for you and help them to discover their untapped potential. Offer them stretch assignments, additional training and unexpected opportunities to lead.
11. Learn the name of the person you are speaking with and use it. In phone conversations, at the beginning of an email and in meeting, make it a point to call someone by their name, it shows that you are paying attention and that you value them.

12. Send handwritten notes or greeting cards to celebrate with your employees. An easy way to send out birthday cards is sign all the cards at the beginning of the month, and then put the date where the stamp goes. Then you can keep track of when to mail them and the stamp covers the date. People will marvel at your memory and thoughtfulness.

Wright

What are the Attributes of Caring?

Willis

What does care look like to the employee? Intrigued by the question, I asked several people to tell me what words they would use to describe a caring leader. Note, asking about a caring leader vs a caring person is critical. We may receive a different answer if we asked just about a person's ability to give care. Here is the list, and there are few, if any, surprise words:

- Appreciative
- Authentic
- Collaborative
- Comfortable
- Compassion
- Compromising
- Friendly
- Good listener
- Respectful
- Thoughtful
- Trusting
- Understanding

Look at this list and see how well you fare on it. Ask yourself where you can do more and think about who you need to spend more time with. Small changes can make a big difference.

Now that we understand the attributes of care, let's look at the opposite, the attributes of those leaders who do not demonstrate care. What does that look like and feel like to the recipient?

- Aloof
- Commanding
- Controlling
- Demeaning
- Egotistical
- Intimidating
- Status seeker
- Untrustworthy

How many of these attributes are you guilty of performing? You may not even recognize that you are doing these things, so it is recommended that you get someone who will give you honest feedback to let you know when you slip into some of these negative behaviors.

The attributes that associates indicated were caring attributes of leaders are not difficult characteristics to put into practice every day. Leaders should make a list and at the end of the week, write down incidents were they demonstrated these behaviors. Doing this exercise for three months should show them how they are or are not progressing. Ideally, the more they demonstrate these behaviors, the more engaged and productive their employees should become.

To **C**onstantly **A**cknowledge and **R**ecognize **E**mployees takes very little time out of a leaders' day. Take five minutes, show someone that you care and your ROI will soar.

Care is the new four-letter word that should be in every leader's vocabulary. Put it in yours today and see what a difference it can make in your organization.

About the Author

Valarie Willis is an accomplished speaker ,consultant, author, and facilitator who understands the complexity of business. With humor and a commitment to helping organizations solve problems, Valarie has built a reputation as a powerful, thought-provoking speaker who brings relevant messages to audiences.

Her passion: to ignite organizations. *Her goal:* to help people at all levels develop their capacity for personal leadership, branding, customer experiences, innovation and creativity.

Throughout her career Valarie has held management, leadership and consulting roles of significant scope.

Author of *Words for Women — from A to Z*, Valarie has an MBA from Xavier University and a B.A. from Wilmington College.

Valarie Willis
P.O. Box 498902
Cincinnati, OH 45249
513-677-5637 (p)
513-677-9945 (f)
vwillis@cinci.rr.com
www.valariewillisconsulting.com

Valarie Willis

Chapter 12

Lethia Owens

David Wright (Wright)

Today we're talking to Lethia Owens, founder and CEO of Lethia Owens International, Inc. Lethia is internationally known as a certified Personal Branding Strategist and leadership expert. She has been sought out by industry leaders in the speaking, transportation, financial services, insurance, banking, technology, legal and aerospace industries for her coaching, consulting and speaking services.

Lethia Owens is regarded as:
- An inspiration to Professionals
- A success Advisor to Solopreneurs
- A growth Strategist to Consultants
- A mentor of Leaders and
- A coach to Super Achievers

Her speaking style is dynamic and she delivers practical, high value content with the amazing ability to engage audiences in a way that makes her message stick. She is the only certified Personal Branding Strategist who specializes in working with speakers to build their million dollar brand. She is the founder of the International Personal Branding and Marketing Association, a member of the National Association of Female Executives

193

(NAFE), the National Speakers Association (NSA), the American Society for Training & Development (ASTD) and she is a national African American Women's Leadership Institute Fellow. Lethia, welcome to Leading the Way to Success.

Lethia Owens (Owens)

Thank you, David, for the opportunity; it's my pleasure.

Wright

So, how would you define success?

Owens

Success is commonly defined in terms of status, money, possessions, achievements and positional power. When one buys into this definition, they often find themselves feeling hopeless, frustrated or anxious because of the tendency to compare their lives to the lives of others. The strategies I will share in this chapter are focused on helping people achieve a kind of success characterized by the following:

- Having an abundance of love, peace and wealth in your life to provide for the emotional, spiritual, financial and physical needs of you and your family.
- Setting and achieving your goals in spite of life's obstacles.
- Breaking through barriers that once held you back.
- Overcoming fear and stepping into your phenomenal future.
- Knowing and loving who you are and sharing it with the world.
- Passionately pursing your purpose as a means to creating your leadership legacy
- Demonstrating your value by using your gifts and talents everyday to make a positive difference in your work.

I believe success as a leader is the extent to which you build a legacy that will live on beyond your existence. Your charge as a leader is to transform the environment into one where employees are excited to come to work. Your aim is to compel people to go beyond what is expected or asked to help the organization be even more profitable and successful.

When you are able to transform the mindset of the people working for and with you such that they, too, see and understand the vision, become committed to it and give all of their energy and attention to helping it become a reality - then you are a success.

Wright

So what is a leadership legacy?

Owens

A leadership legacy is the mark you leave in the minds and hearts of those who have followed you. Your legacy as a leader is comprised of the collective thoughts, feelings, ideas and perceptions of who you are and what you stand for. I often ask my coaching clients this question: "When you leave your position, what will people say about your leadership?" This is part of the process used to help them become more intentional about building a leadership legacy worthy of remark. The goal in building your leadership legacy is to lead in such a way that your impact continues far beyond your positional appointment.

Coaching Questions:
- If I were to interview people who work for you, and ask them to describe you in one sentence, what would they say?
- How do you feel about their perception of you?

Wright

What is the Leadership Branding Model?

Owens

Building your leadership legacy requires that you become intentional about the brand you are building. As you build your leadership brand you will discover that it is the foundation upon which your legacy will be built. The leadership brand model is made up of three distinct phases.

Wright

So what are the three distinct phases of the Leadership Brand Model?

Owens

The Three Phases of the Leadership Brand Model are:

Prepare - Know who you are

Position - Leverage your strengths

Promote – Communicate your brand message

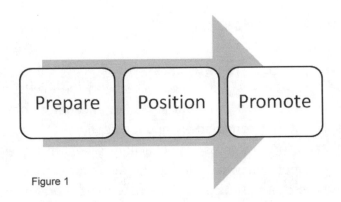

Figure 1

Let's walk through each of these phases to gain a better understanding of the process.

Phase 1 – Prepare: During this phase, you explore your current brand and begin to think about the brand you would like to build. If you want to build a powerful leadership brand, you need to perform the same type of brand research that companies conduct, but on a personal level. The 360° Personal Brand Assessment is a powerful tool that can be used to help research your leadership brand. Readers can visit me online at www.LeadingTheWay2Success.com where they will find lots of valuable resources for building their powerful leadership brand. You identify your personal leadership assets and answer the question, "Why would people want to work for me?" An important step in this phase is identifying "The Gap."

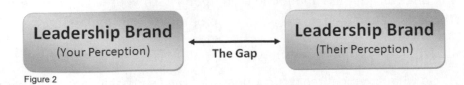

Figure 2

Understanding the brand gap is critical as it helps you clearly see the perception difference of your leadership brand between you and those you work with. Once you become clear on where you are and where you would like to be, you can begin putting a plan in place to position you as a stronger, more powerful brand. That leads us to the next phase.

Phase 2 – Position: During this phase, you begin to craft your leadership brand message using what you learned in the prepare phase so you can begin to position yourself with intention. You start identifying ways to share your brand message. Once you identify who belongs in your target audience, you will formulate a strategic communication plan that allows you to clearly and consistently communicate your brand message so you are congruent. Clarity, consistency and congruence build credibility for your leadership brand.

Phase 3 – Promote: Once you have clarity on your leadership brand message and a strategic communication plan for sharing your brand message, the next step is to promote your brand to your target audience. Today's professionals often hear, "You must learn how to toot your own horn!", yet many do not know how to promote their value and contributions without feeling arrogant. During this phase you identify ways to share your brand message and promote your Unique Promise of Value (UPV) to your organization and direct reports in a way that is authentic to your leadership and communication style.

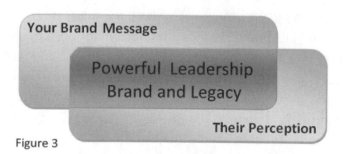

Your Brand Message

Powerful Leadership Brand and Legacy

Their Perception

Figure 3

The result of effectively moving through each of these three phases is a reduction in your brand gap and the revealing of your "Powerful Leadership Brand and Legacy."

Lethia Owens

Coaching Exercises:

1) Consider using a 360° Personal Brand Assessment to analyze your current leadership brand and use the results to help you reduce your brand gap. (Visit www.LeadingTheWay2Success.com and discover lots of valuable resources for building a powerful leadership brand.)

2) Can you articulate what makes you different and unique as a leader? Why would someone want to work for you?

3) Can you articulate what makes you different and unique as a leader? Why would someone want to work for you?

4) What would a powerful leadership brand look like for you?

5) Consider using the following simple, yet informative, monthly report to enhance your supervisor's understanding of your leadership brand. Send a well-crafted email highlighting the following:

   - A list of my accomplishments this month...
   - A list of the challenges I have faced this month...
   - Suggested names for feedback solicitation...
   - What I need from you to help me be even more successful and or effective...

Wright

Reflecting on the "Three Phases of Brand Development," why is it important to get to know who you are during the *prepare* phase?

Owens

Building your powerful leadership brand is not about fabricating a professional image you think will deliver the success you desire. Instead, the power of your brand is ignited by becoming more of who you already are. Believe in yourself. Be who you are on purpose and without apology. Your success and strength lie within, not shaped and released by external forces. Dare to be more of who you are and never imitate someone else. Every great brand is unique. The goal is to identify what makes you unique, different and valuable and then turn up the visibility on these characteristics so more of who you are is seen in your conversations and interactions. What makes you unique is your point of leverage for creating the leadership success you desire. A clear understanding of your brand attributes, strengths and weaknesses gives you the advantage-seeking

198

opportunities that are in alignment with your greatest ability to add value. Be intentional in your professional development by sharing your brand insights with your supervisor and encouraging him or her to partner with you to find more opportunities to bring your strengths to the table and contribute in a more powerful and impactful way. Consistently choosing opportunities that leverage your strengths creates powerful stepping stones to higher levels of success.

Wright

So is leveraging your strengths essential to the second phase, called *position*?

Owens

Yes. Think of it in this way: When you are clear on your Unique Promise of Value (UPV), it becomes easier to find your fit within the organization, thus positioning you for maximum success. While it is critical that you identify your strengths and learn how to use them, it is also important to identify your weaknesses so you can learn to manage them. Several years ago I took an assessment designed by the Gallup organization (the assessment can be found at www.StrengthFinders.com). This assessment reveals an individual's strengths as identified by the top five signature themes. Well, my #1 theme is Activator, which equates to, "Let's make something happen!" My 32nd out of 34 themes is Empathy. Once I discovered this I immediately said to myself, "That explains a lot." You see, I have become clear on ways I can use my Activator theme to help me create phenomenal success and yet I have had to learn how to manage my lack of empathy so that it no longer undermines my ability to inspire people to move forward and accomplish the vision and mission at hand. Work can be so much more enjoyable and rewarding when we find our fit, become energized by our contributions and bring passion to work with us. We become engaged leaders who develop engaged followers who are positioned for greater success.

Wright

I asked a friend of mine the other day how many people worked for him. He had twenty employees in his company; yet he responded, "About half of them." This is probably his standard answer, but it's really not funny when you think about it in this day and time. So how can a leader motivate and inspire their team to be more productive?

Owens

I think it starts with the leader's ability to inspire and motivate their team to give more than is requested. So you may be thinking, "So how exactly does one do this?"

When a leader has successfully moved through the *prepare* and *position* phases, they being to transform their work environment. Their confidence level increases and their excitement for their work begins to increase. As they become intentional during the *promote* phase, the passion and energy they bring to their work is contagious and starts to rub off on even the most unlikely individuals.

Wright

So, overall, how important is a leadership brand and legacy when leading others?

Owens

One of the greatest rewards of leadership is the opportunity to see yourself as dream broker. As a leader, your success, and ultimately the leadership legacy you build, will be based on how good you become at brokering dreams. In order to become a dream broker, you must first understand the dreams, goals, talents, and gifts of the people you lead and the people within your sphere of influence. By doing so, you help others find their own path to success and you help your team members find their fit within the organization; therefore, they, too, are empowered to reach their highest potential.

Leaders who shout directives instead of providing direction gain little respect from those who follow them. Leaders who shout, "You matter!" gain more than a follower – they gain a partner on their journey towards success.

The late Charles Schultz, creator of the Peanuts comic strip, once posed a series of questions to help readers reflect on the truly important things in life. It was in Reader's Digest but I haven't been able to find the exact reference. The exercise is a powerful one, so I'd like to pose these same questions to you:

Step 1: Can you remember the names of the last five winners of:

- The Heisman Trophy?
- The Miss America Pageant?
- The Academy Award for best actor or actress?

Step 2: Now, can you remember the names of five:

- People whose stories most inspired you?
- Teachers who most influenced you?
- Friends who have help you most?

Most people can only recall a few of the answers for Step 1, even though the individuals have all been household names at one time. But when asked the questions in Step 2, Schultz found that people could quickly name the people who have most impacted their lives. These individuals come quickly to mind because they once encouraged, inspired, motivated, trusted, or believed in us. They have served as coaches, leaders, guides, and partners on our personal or professional journey.

Who will remember the contributions you have made? Whose life will be saved, transformed, inspired, or changed because of your leadership? Your decision to intentionally create a leadership legacy will positively impact others now and for future generations.

Today you drink from wells you did not dig, benefit from corporate initiatives you did not implement, and walk through doors you did not open, all because of the positive and powerful legacy of someone before you. Leaders who build powerful leadership legacies demonstrate certain competencies and skills that aide in their ability to make a lasting impact on the people they work with and the organizations they serve. When you lead with an energetic, visionary, and open attitude based on clear values, you create an environment that makes it possible for employees to truly leverage their talents and skills. In this type of environment, they know they will be appreciated. This positive work environment motivates associates to take responsibility for their actions and personal growth.

I believe there are five essential components to building a positive leadership legacy and they are - Credibility, Communication and Coaching.

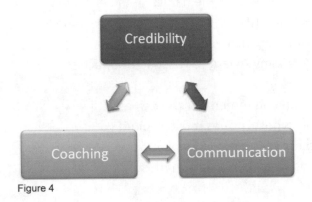

Figure 4

Coaching Question:
1) What might you do differently to better encourage, support and lead your team?
2) What might you do to establish more credibility with your team?
3) What might you do to communicate more effectively as a leader?
4) What role can coaching play to help you develop your team?

Your credibility will be established as a by-product of your character and your character is not what you say, but what you do. Effective leadership is about doing the right things right at the right time.

In studying the lives of many great leaders including Mary Kay Ash, Mother Teresa, and John Maxwell, I have found that regardless of the issue, challenge, and possible personal gain or loss, they always did the right thing. Not occasionally, nor most of the time, but always did the right thing. Their demonstration of character was consistent and contagious. The power derived from their unwavering commitment to doing the right thing compelled others to follow in their footsteps and to commit to their dreams.

Your passion for the work at hand will serve as your greatest tool to inspire and encourage your team during demanding and challenging times. Your enthusiasm for the project and your attitude when faced with adversity will nurture your team's need for guidance and motivation.

- Ask yourself, "Am I passionate about my work?" If you're not, how can you expect your staff to be passionate about their work?
- If you don't feel inspired, if you don't feel fired up about coming to work, do some soul searching and find out why.
- Are you simply tired or overloaded and therefore "running on empty?" If so, understand it's hard to get excited about anything when you are running on fumes.
- Do you no longer feel connected to your organization's mission or do you even feel at odds with it?
- Does your job or profession no longer enliven you? Or, have you simply been running on autopilot and now do you need to reconnect with what you love about your work and the value you and your organization provide?

Whatever the source of your lack inspiration, you need to rekindle your passion in order for your people to be inspired and motivated. With established creditability and a passion for your work you will be in a position to accomplish great things through the powers of influence and persuasion. The two are great partners and are actually more effective than the inherent positional power that comes with the titles of leadership.

Wright

What communication strategies are essential to effective leadership?

Owens

I have been hired by Fortune 500 companies around the world from Dallas to Dubai to help their employees and leaders build powerful personal brands; yet I have never been hired to help people "talk more." I have, however, been hired numerous times to help professionals learn how to listen more. Listening is a skill that is often underutilized and has negative consequences of neglect. Considering what we have learned about building a leadership legacy, it should be clear that seeking to understand the gifts, talents and strengths of employees will improve one's ability to manage and lead their team. Listening is one of the tools leaders use to help identify their employees' strengths and opportunities to add value. Effective leaders will incorporate what they learn about their employees to shape their communication when sharing their vision. They paint a picture of success that features the employee in a starring role - a role the employee is excited to play. You know, people get really excited when they can see themselves in the big picture representing something powerful and positive.

Wright

So what role does coaching play in the success of a leader?

Owens

Coaching your employees so they can improve their performance is a key component to leaving a leadership legacy. Coaching is about creating an environment wherein people can grow. Top performers need to learn new skills and develop new ideas in order to work at their peaks. People who learn new things, work with diverse groups of people, and are given the opportunity to experience different roles that expand their worldview produce a richer organization. These skills and attributes help create people who respect differences, people who are more self-assured, who listen well, and are more curious.

As a leader, you have the power to influence people and therefore influence their performance. If you believe in creating an environment through coaching where trust, optimism, enjoyment, and personal growth are encouraged, then you will build a sustainable, high-performing team— and, in the process, create many new leaders.

Wright

Why is it important to leverage the power of collaboration on one's journey to leadership success?

Owens

I believe that collaboration is the fastest path to success, and isolation is the fastest path to insanity. Try to do everything all by yourself and you will eventually go crazy or burnout. Leaders are able to accomplish much more when they learn to leverage the talents and gifts of others. Delegation is a powerful tool for both developing the leadership abilities of your team and managing your workload. Always look for opportunities to use collaboration to encourage employees to support one another.

Collaboration is the way that we all can win because if we are all supporting and encouraging each other, then at the end of the day, the work gets done and we all feel better about an opportunity to spend most of our day operating out of our strengths and less of our time operating out of our weaknesses.

Wright

Wow, Lethia, you were chosen to go into this book on leadership simply because of your ability to deliver high value content in a really practical way and I appreciate your doing that for us today, and I appreciate your taking all of this time to answer all of these questions about building a leadership brand and legacy.

Owens

Oh, it's my pleasure, David! Thank you so much for the opportunity. I'd like to close our interview with an anonymous poem that inspires me every single day:

A cautious leader I must be, for a future leader follows me.
I do not dare go astray, for fear they'll go the same self way.
I cannot once escape their eyes, for what they see me do they try.
Like me one day they say they'll be, the future leader who follows me.
So I must remember as I go, through
exhilarating highs and discouraging lows.
That I am building for all to see, the future leader who follows me.

Wright

Today we're talking to Lethia Owens. She is the founder and CEO of Lethia Owens International, Inc. She is internationally known as a certified Personal Branding Strategist and leadership expert and is regarded as an inspiration to professionals, success advisor to solopreneurs, growth strategist to consultants, mentor of leaders and coach to super achievers. Lethia thank you so much for being with us today on Leading The Way To Success.

Owens

Thank you for the opportunity David. I encourage readers to visit me online at www.LeadingTheWay2Success.com where they will find lots of valuable resources for building their leadership brand.

About the Author

Lethia Owens is the president and CEO of Lethia Owens International, Inc. Mrs. Owens is a certified personal branding strategist, information-technology expert and business authority with more than 16 years of leadership experience and a strong track record of results. She is a highly sought out international speaker, coach, author and consultant to many fortune 500 companies, churches and non-profit organizations.

She has traveled the world from Dallas to Dubai teaching people how to unearth their passions, realize their potential and embrace their phenomenal future. As a messenger of hope, she helps others discover possibilities, develop strategies, plan purposefully and execute diligently. She uses her high value content, dynamic keynote presentations and engaging training programs to show others they too can achieve extraordinary results – if they are authentic in their pursuit of purpose and develop a strategy for communicating their unique value to others. Through the use of real-life stories and common sense strategies, she awakens the potential in clients and audiences to think, work and live powerfully. Her enthusiasm is contagious and she has the amazing ability to engage audiences in a way that allows them to envision new possibilities and eagerly anticipate future successes.

Lethia has worked with Fortune 500 companies in the Insurance, Financial Services, Telecommunication, Oil Refinery, Transportation, Healthcare, Aerospace and Defense, Non-profit, Technology, Legal and Medical industries. Mrs. Owens has delivered more than 350 presentations, facilitated over 800 coaching sessions and has extensive experience in leadership development, strategic planning and personal branding.

Lethia is the Founder and Chartering President of the International Personal Branding and Marketing Association and she is a member of the National Speakers Association, the American Society for Training and Development, the National African-American Women's Leadership Institute and the National Association of Female Executives.

Lethia Owens
513 River Bend Estates Drive
St. Charles, Mo
636.244.5041
Lethia@LethiaOwens.com
www.LethiaOwens.com
www.LeadingTheWay2Success.com

Chapter 13

Jack Canfield

David E. Wright (Wright)

Today we are talking with Jack Canfield. You probably know him as the founder and co-creator of the *New York Times* number one bestselling *Chicken Soup for the Soul* book series. As of 2006 there are sixty-five titles and eighty million copies in print in over thirty-seven languages.

Jack's background includes a BA from Harvard, a master's from the University of Massachusetts, and an Honorary Doctorate from the University of Santa Monica. He has been a high school and university teacher, a workshop facilitator, a psychotherapist, and a leading authority in the area of self-esteem and personal development.

Jack Canfield, welcome to *Leading the Way to Success.*

Jack Canfield (Canfield)

Thank you, David. It's great to be with you.

Wright

I talked with Mark Victor Hansen a few days ago. He gave you full credit for coming up with the idea of the *Chicken Soup* series. Obviously it's made you an internationally known personality. Other than recognition, has the series changed you personally and if so, how?

Canfield

I would say that it has and I think in a couple of ways. Number one, I read stories all day long of people who've overcome what would feel like insurmountable obstacles. For example, we just did a book *Chicken Soup for the Unsinkable Soul*. There's a story in there about a single mother with three daughters. She contracted a disease and she had to have both of her hands and both of her feet amputated. She got prosthetic devices and was able to learn how to use them. She could cook, drive the car, brush her daughters' hair, get a job, etc. I read that and I thought, "God, what would I ever have to complain and whine and moan about?"

At one level it's just given me a great sense of gratitude and appreciation for everything I have and it has made me less irritable about the little things.

I think the other thing that's happened for me personally is my sphere of influence has changed. By that I mean I was asked, for example, a couple of years ago to be the keynote speaker to the Women's Congressional Caucus. The Caucus is a group that includes all women in America who are members of Congress and who are state senators, governors, and lieutenant governors. I asked what they wanted me to talk about—what topic.

"Whatever you think we need to know to be better legislators," was the reply.

I thought, "Wow, they want me to tell them about what laws they should be making and what would make a better culture." Well, that wouldn't have happened if our books hadn't come out and I hadn't become famous. I think I get to play with people at a higher level and have more influence in the world. That's important to me because my life purpose is inspiring and empowering people to live their highest vision so the world works for everybody. I get to do that on a much bigger level than when I was just a high school teacher back in Chicago.

Wright

I think one of the powerful components of that book series is that you can read a positive story in just a few minutes and come back and revisit it. I know my daughter has three of the books and she just reads them interchangeably. Sometimes I go in her bedroom and she'll be crying and reading one of them. Other times she'll be laughing, so they really are "chicken soup for the soul," aren't they?

Canfield

They really are. In fact we have four books in the *Teenage Soul* series now and a new one coming out at the end of this year. I have a son who's eleven and he has a twelve-year-old friend who's a girl. We have a new book called *Chicken Soup for the Teenage Soul and the Tough Stuff*. It's all about dealing with parents' divorces, teachers who don't understand you, boyfriends who drink and drive, and other issues pertinent to that age group.

I asked my son's friend, "Why do you like this book?" (It's our most popular book among teens right now.) She said, "You know, whenever I'm feeling down I read it and it makes me cry and I feel better. Some of the stories make me laugh and some of the stories make me feel more responsible for my life. But basically I just feel like I'm not alone."

One of the people I work with recently said that the books are like a support group between the covers of a book—you can read about other peoples' experiences and realize you're not the only one going through something.

Wright

Jack, we're trying to encourage people in our audience to be better, to live better, and be more fulfilled by reading about the experiences of our writers. Is there anyone or anything in your life that has made a difference for you and helped you to become a better person?

Canfield

Yes, and we could do ten books just on that. I'm influenced by people all the time. If I were to go way back I'd have to say one of the key influences in my life was Jesse Jackson when he was still a minister in Chicago. I was teaching in an all black high school there and I went to Jesse Jackson's church with a friend one time. What happened for me was that I saw somebody with a vision. (This was before Martin Luther King was killed and Jesse was of the lieutenants in his organization.) I just saw people trying to make the world work better for a certain segment of the population. I was inspired by that kind of visionary belief that it's possible to make change.

Later on, John F. Kennedy was a hero of mine. I was very much inspired by him.

Another is a therapist by the name of Robert Resnick. He was my therapist for two years. He taught me a little formula: E + R = O. It stands for Events + Response = Outcome. He said, "If you don't like your outcomes quit blaming the events and start changing your responses." One of his favorite phrases was,

"If the grass on the other side of the fence looks greener, start watering your own lawn more."

I think he helped me get off any kind of self-pity I might have had because I had parents who were alcoholics. It would have been very easy to blame them for problems I might have had. They weren't very successful or rich; I was surrounded by people who were and I felt like, "God, what if I'd had parents like they had? I could have been a lot better." He just got me off that whole notion and made me realize that the hand you were dealt is the hand you've got to play. Take responsibility for who you are and quit complaining and blaming others and get on with your life. That was a turning point for me.

I'd say the last person who really affected me big-time was a guy named W. Clement Stone who was a self-made multi-millionaire in Chicago. He taught me that success is not a four-letter word—it's nothing to be ashamed of—and you ought to go for it. He said, "The best thing you can do for the poor is not be one of them." Be a model for what it is to live a successful life. So I learned from him the principles of success and that's what I've been teaching now for more than thirty years.

Wright

He was an entrepreneur in the insurance industry, wasn't he?

Canfield

He was. He had combined insurance. When I worked for him he was worth 600 million dollars and that was before the dot.com millionaires came along in Silicon Valley. He just knew more about success. He was a good friend of Napoleon Hill (author of *Think and Grow Rich)* and he was a fabulous mentor. I really learned a lot from him.

Wright

I miss some of the men I listened to when I was a young salesman coming up and he was one of them. Napoleon Hill was another one as was Dr. Peale. All of their writings made me who I am today. I'm glad I had that opportunity.

Canfield

One speaker whose name you probably will remember, Charlie "Tremendous" Jones, says, "Who we are is a result of the books we read and the people we hang out with." I think that's so true and that's why I tell people, "If you want to have high self-esteem, hang out with people who have high self-esteem. If you want to be more spiritual, hang out with spiritual people." We're always telling our children, "Don't hang out with those kids." The reason we don't want them to is because we know how influential people are with each other. I think we need to give ourselves the same advice. Who are we hanging out with? We can hang out with them in books, cassette tapes, CDs, radio shows, and in person.

Wright

One of my favorites was a fellow named Bill Gove from Florida. I talked with him about three or four years ago. He's retired now. His mind is still as quick as it ever was. I thought he was one of the greatest speakers I had ever heard.

What do you think makes up a great mentor? In other words, are there characteristics that mentors seem to have in common?

Canfield

I think there are two obvious ones. I think mentors have to have the time to do it and the willingness to do it. I also think they need to be people who are doing something you want to do. W. Clement Stone used to tell me, "If you want to be rich, hang out with rich people. Watch what they do, eat what they eat, dress the way they dress—try it on." He wasn't suggesting that you give up your authentic self, but he was pointing out that rich people probably have habits that you don't have and you should study them.

I always ask salespeople in an organization, "Who are the top two or three in your organization?" I tell them to start taking them out to lunch and dinner and for a drink and finding out what they do. Ask them, "What's your secret?" Nine times out of ten they'll be willing to tell you.

This goes back to what we said earlier about asking. I'll go into corporations and I'll say, "Who are the top ten people?" They'll all tell me and I'll say, "Did you ever ask them what they do different than you?"

"No," they'll reply.

"Why not?"

"Well, they might not want to tell me."

"How do you know? Did you ever ask them? All they can do is say no. You'll be no worse off than you are now."

So I think with mentors you just look at people who seem to be living the life you want to live and achieving the results you want to achieve.

What we say in our book is when that you approach a mentor they're probably busy and successful and so they haven't got a lot of time. Just ask,

"Can I talk to you for ten minutes every month?" If I know it's only going to be ten minutes I'll probably say yes. The neat thing is if I like you I'll always give you more than ten minutes, but that ten minutes gets you in the door.

Wright

In the future are there any more Jack Canfield books authored singularly?

Canfield

One of my books includes the formula I mentioned earlier: $E + R = O$. I just felt I wanted to get that out there because every time I give a speech and I talk about that the whole room gets so quiet you could hear a pin drop—I can tell people are really getting value.

Then I'm going to do a series of books on the principles of success. I've got about 150 of them that I've identified over the years. I have a book down the road I want to do that's called *No More Put-Downs,* which is a book probably aimed mostly at parents, teachers, and managers. There's a culture we have now of put-down humor. Whether it's *Married . . . with Children* or *All in the Family,* there's that characteristic of macho put-down humor. There's research now showing how bad it is for kids' self-esteem when the coaches do it, so I want to get that message out there as well.

Wright

It's really not that funny, is it?

Canfield

No, we'll laugh it off because we don't want to look like we're a wimp but underneath we're hurt. The research now shows that you're better off breaking a child's bones than you are breaking their spirit. A bone will heal much more quickly than their emotional spirit will.

Wright

I remember recently reading a survey where people listed the top five people who had influenced them. I've tried it on a couple of groups at church and in other places. In my case, and in the survey, approximately three out of the top five are always teachers. I wonder if that's going to be the same in the next decade.

Canfield

I think that's probably because as children we're at our most formative years. We actually spend more time with our teachers than we do with our parents. Research shows that the average parent only interacts verbally with each of their children only about eight and a half minutes a day. Yet at school they're interacting with their teachers for anywhere from six to eight hours depending on how long the school day is, including coaches, chorus directors, etc.

I think that in almost everybody's life there's been that one teacher who loved him or her as a human being—an individual—not just one of the many students the teacher was supposed to fill full of History and English. That teacher believed in you and inspired you.

Les Brown is one of the great motivational speakers in the world. If it hadn't been for one teacher who said, "I think you can do more than be in a special education class. I think you're the one," he'd probably still be cutting grass in the median strip of the highways in Florida instead of being a $35,000-a-talk speaker.

Wright

I had a conversation one time with Les. He told me about this wonderful teacher who discovered Les was dyslexic. Everybody else called him dumb and this one lady just took him under her wing and had him tested. His entire life changed because of her interest in him.

Canfield

I'm on the board of advisors of the Dyslexic Awareness Resource Center here in Santa Barbara. The reason is because I taught high school and had a lot of kids who were called "at-risk"—kids who would end up in gangs and so forth.

What we found over and over was that about 78 percent of all the kids in the juvenile detention centers in Chicago were kids who had learning disabilities—primarily dyslexia—but there were others as well. They were never diagnosed and they weren't doing well in school so they'd drop out. As soon as a student drops out of school he or she becomes subject to the influence of gangs and other kinds of criminal and drug linked activities. If these kids had been diagnosed earlier we'd have been able to get rid of a large amount of the juvenile crime in America because there are a lot of really good programs that can teach dyslexics to read and excel in school.

Wright

My wife is a teacher and she brings home stories that are heartbreaking about parents not being as concerned with their children as they used to be, or at least not as helpful as they used to be. Did you find that to be a problem when you were teaching?

Canfield

It depends on what kind of district you're in. If it's a poor district the parents could be on drugs, alcoholics, and basically just not available. If you're in a really high rent district the parents are not available because they're both working, coming home tired, they're jet-setters, or they're working late at the office because they're workaholics. Sometimes it just legitimately takes two paychecks to pay the rent anymore.

I find that the majority of parents care but often they don't know what to do. They don't know how to discipline their children. They don't know how to help them with their homework. They can't pass on skills that they never acquired themselves.

Unfortunately, the trend tends to be like a chain letter. The people with the least amount of skills tend to have the most number of children. The other thing is that you get crack babies (infants born addicted to crack cocaine because of the mother's addiction). As of this writing, in Los Angeles one out of every ten babies born is a crack baby.

Wright

That's unbelievable.

Canfield

Yes, and another statistic is that by the time 50 percent of the kids are twelve years old they have started experimenting with alcohol. I see a lot of that in the Bible belt. The problem is not the big city, urban designer drugs, but alcoholism.

Another thing you get, unfortunately, is a lot of let's call it "familial violence"—kids getting beat up, parents who drink and then explode, child abuse, and sexual abuse. You see a lot of that.

Wright

Most people are fascinated by these television shows about being a survivor. What has been the greatest comeback that you have made from adversity in your career or in your life?

Canfield

You know, it's funny, I don't think I've had a lot of major failures and setbacks where I had to start over. My life's been on an intentional curve. But I do have a lot of challenges. Mark and I are always setting goals that challenge us. We always say, "The purpose of setting a really big goal is not so that you can achieve it so much, but it's who you become in the process of achieving it." A friend of mine, Jim Rohn, says, "You want to set goals big enough so that in the process of achieving them you become someone worth being."

I think that to be a millionaire is nice but so what? People make the money and then they lose it. People get the big houses and then they burn down or Silicon Valley goes belly up and all of a sudden they don't have a big house anymore. But who you became in the process of learning how to be successful can never be taken away from you. So what we do is constantly put big challenges in front of us.

We have a book called *Chicken Soup for the Teacher's Soul.* (You'll have to make sure to get a copy for your wife.) I was a teacher and a teacher trainer for years. But because of the success of the *Chicken Soup* books I haven't been in the education world that much. I've got to go out and relearn how I market to that world. I met with a Superintendent of Schools. I met with a guy named Jason Dorsey who's one of the number one consultants in the world in that area. I found out who has the bestselling book in that area. I sat down with his wife for a day and talked about her marketing approaches.

I believe that if you face any kind of adversity, whether it's losing your job, your spouse dies, you get divorced, you're in an accident like Christopher Reeve and become paralyzed, or whatever, you simply do what you have to do. You find out who's already handled the problem and how did they've handled it. Then you get the support you need to get through it by their example. Whether it's a counselor in your church or you go on a retreat or you read the Bible, you do something that gives you the support you need to get to the other end.

You also have to know what the end is that you want to have. Do you want to be remarried? Do you just want to have a job and be a single mom? What is it? If you reach out and ask for support I think you'll get help. People really like to help other people. They're not always available because sometimes they're going through problems also; but there's always someone with a helping hand.

Often I think we let our pride get in the way. We let our stubbornness get in the way. We let our belief in how the world should be interfere and get in our way instead of dealing with how the world is. When we get that out of that way then we can start doing that which we need to do to get where we need to go.

Wright

If you could have a platform and tell our audience something you feel that would help or encourage them, what would you say?

Canfield

I'd say number one is to believe in yourself, believe in your dreams, and trust your feelings. I think too many people are trained wrong when they're little kids. For example, when kids are mad at their daddy they're told, "You're not mad at your Daddy."

They say, "Gee, I thought I was."

Or the kid says, "That's going to hurt," and the doctor says, "No it's not." Then they give you the shot and it hurts. They say, "See that didn't hurt, did it?" When that happened to you as a kid, you started to not trust yourself.

You may have asked your mom, "Are you upset?" and she says, "No," but she really was. So you stop learning to trust your perception.

I tell this story over and over. There are hundreds of people I've met who've come from upper class families where they make big incomes and the dad's a doctor. The kid wants to be a mechanic and work in an auto shop because that's what he loves. The family says, "That's beneath us. You can't do that." So the kid ends up being an anesthesiologist killing three people because he's not paying attention. What he really wants to do is tinker with cars.

I tell people you've got to trust your own feelings, your own motivations, what turns you on, what you want to do, what makes you feel good, and quit worrying about what other people say, think, and want for you. Decide what you want for yourself and then do what you need to do to go about getting it. It takes work.

I read a book a week minimum and at the end of the year I've read fifty-two books. We're talking about professional books—books on self-help, finances, psychology, parenting, and so forth. At the end of ten years I've read 520 books. That puts me in the top 1 percent of people knowing important information in this country. But most people are spending their time watching television.

When I went to work for W. Clement Stone, he told me, "I want you to cut out one hour a day of television."

"Okay," I said, "what do I do with it?"

"Read," he said.

He told me what kind of books to read. He said, "At the end of a year you'll have spent 365 hours reading. Divide that by a forty-hour work week and that's nine and a half weeks of education every year."

I thought, "Wow, that's two months." It was like going back to summer school.

As a result of his advice I have close to 8,000 books in my library. The reason I'm involved in this book project instead of someone else is that people like me, Jim Rohn, Les Brown, and you read a lot. We listen to tapes and we go to seminars. That's why we're the people with the information.

I always say that your raise becomes effective when you do. You'll become more effective as you gain more skills, more insight, and more knowledge.

Wright

Jack, I have watched your career for over a decade and your accomplishments are just outstanding. But your humanitarian efforts are really what impress me. I think that you're doing great things not only in California, but all over the country.

Canfield

It's true. In addition to all of the work we do, we pick one to three charities and we've given away over six million dollars in the last eight years, along with our publisher who matches every penny we give away. We've planted over a million trees in Yosemite National Park. We've bought hundreds of thousands of cataract operations in third world countries. We've contributed to the Red Cross, the Humane Society, and on it goes. It feels like a real blessing to be able to make that kind of a contribution to the world.

Wright

Today we have been talking with Jack Canfield, founder and co-creator of the *Chicken Soup for the Soul* book series. As of 2006, there are sixty-five titles and eighty million copies in print in over thirty-seven languages.

Canfield

Another book is *The Success Principles*. In it I share sixty-four principles that other people and I have utilized to achieve great levels of success.

In 2002 we published *Chicken Soup for the Soul of America*. It includes stories that grew out of 9/11 and is a real healing book for our nation. I would encourage readers to get a copy and share it with their families.

Wright

I will stand in line to get one of those. Thank you so much being with us.

About the Author

Jack Canfield is one of America's leading experts on developing self-esteem and peak performance. A dynamic and entertaining speaker, as well as a highly sought-after trainer, he has a wonderful ability to inform and inspire audiences toward developing their own human potential and personal effectiveness.

Jack Canfield is most well-known for the *Chicken Soup for the Soul* series, which he co-authored with Mark Victor Hansen, and for his audio programs about building high self-esteem. Jack is the founder of Self-Esteem Seminars, located in Santa Barbara, California, which trains entrepreneurs, educators, corporate leaders, and employees how to accelerate the achievement of their personal and professional goals. Jack is also founder of The Foundation for Self Esteem, located in Culver City, California, which provides self-esteem resources and training to social workers, welfare recipients, and human resource professionals.

Jack graduated from Harvard in 1966, received his ME degree at the University of Massachusetts in 1973, and earned an Honorary Doctorate from the University of Santa Monica. He has been a high school and university teacher, a workshop facilitator, a psychotherapist, and a leading authority in the area of self-esteem and personal development.

As a result of his work with prisoners, welfare recipients, and inner-city youth, Jack was appointed by the State Legislature to the California Task Force to Promote Self-Esteem and Personal and Social Responsibility. He also served on the Board of Trustees of the National Council for Self-Esteem.

Jack Canfield
Worldwide Headquarters
The Jack Canfield Companies
P.O. Box 30880
Santa Barbara, CA 93130
805.563.2935
www.jackcanfield.com

Jack Canfield

Chapter 14

Jennifer Sabin

David Wright (Wright)

Today we are talking with Jennifer Sabin. Jennifer is the Founder and Managing Partner of the Growth Management Group LLC. For more than twenty years she has been an industry leader providing premium coaching and consulting services in more than twenty-three countries. She started out in the '80s as the youngest woman owning an American Stock Exchange seat and she rapidly expanded her firm into a premier international consulting and coaching company. She is deeply committed to the success of her clients from corporate to private individuals. In addition to working directly with many of the GMG clients, she is a renowned speaker and lecturer and has addressed groups from New York to Taipei to Moscow.

Jennifer is also the lead creative and program designer on the GMG LLC design team for workshops, programs, seminars, and private client work. She delivers programs that are always on the cutting edge of combining the philosophy of coaching and the pragmatism and expertise of business. Jennifer is the recipient of numerous awards including the New York Mayor's Volunteer Service Award for her consulting work with businesses impacted by the U.S. tragedy on September 11. She served Girls Inc, National Advisory Board for Economic Literacy, she sat on the Congressional Organized Market 2000 Committee, and was invited to attend the 21st Century Summit in Washington D.C., where she and other business leaders met with the President and discussed issues affecting women entrepreneurs. Jennifer has been recognized by the National Association of Women Business Owners (NAWBO) at their national conference as a Tale of Triumph.

Jennifer welcome to *Leading the Way to Success.*

Jennifer Sabin (Sabin)

Thank you. It is a pleasure to be here.

Wright

Given your broad experience in working with clients from many different cultural and economic constructs where is the most beneficial place to begin in approaching *Leading the Way to Success?*

Sabin

A wise place to start is to establish a shared definition. In this topic there are three key words: Leading, Way and Success. First is Leading, essentially providing direction or guidance. Way is the route from one place to another: it's the manner or method. Success is fulfilling an identified objective. For our conversation "Leading the Way to Success" is a person or perhaps a group in the forefront, providing direction and guidance on the route and manner to an identified and desired objective .The purpose is to fulfill on that objective. Simple to define, and yet living it is not simple.

Wright

It is a best practice for many organizations and academics to begin with commonly understood language. It seems as though this process can help to minimize misunderstandings and miscommunications. Is this an approach that you typically use?

Sabin

David, this is such a rich wonderful topic and it is important that the experiences and the information be relevant and valuable.

The magnitude of information, opinions and material on Leading, Leadership and Success is vast and overwhelming: books, periodicals, tapes, seminars and the web. *Leading the Way to Success* can fall into the deep dark abyss of jargon. The layers of jargon and the quantity of resources can truly disconnect us from the power of this language, what it actually means. Leading the Way to Success is an incredibly potent phrase that can transform lives and the experience of self. Taking time for clarity on the definition is fundamental and critical. This is about leading and I believe every man and woman can be leading the way to success. Leading in this context is inclusive not exclusive.

My focus today is actually not on leaders. It is on leading and there is a distinction. A primary component of leading is having an identified objective and dedicating our time, energy and resources to achieving it— we name it and we go to claim it! Think about the potent simplicity. When we have a goal and are on the way to achieving it, we are Leading the Way to Success. In this approach to Leading, there is the opportunity for each of to emerge as a leader and to demonstrate qualities of leadership. This opportunity applies to each of us. It is this simple.

Wright

Am I to understand that you believe that anyone who has an objective and is working on fulfilling upon it is a leader and is Leading the way to success?

Sabin

This topic is not about leaders per se, it is about leading. Leading is not equal to leader with a capital L, as in world Leader, The vast majority of those leading the way to success are not known on a global level or by tens of thousands or even hundreds; these are the men and women in our families, businesses, and communities. They are neighbors, friends, family, co-workers, peers, and so on....and this person who is leading can become a leader.

Every person has the capacity to be leading the way to success. When we take ownership of that ability, an entire universe opens up. Actually, once the myth is peeled away, there is the basic formula that any person can use to be leading and then to discover the leader within them. This journey of discovery happens while leading the way to success, not before.

Jennifer Sabin

Wright

Leading comes before being a leader. You are presenting a perspective that is not in line with the conventional or even traditional view of leaders and leadership. Is this how you approach leadership?

Sabin

In this context yes. Most people are not a leader first by title. In fact, for most of us we have to find someone to share our vision or goal. This is different for a leader by position or title. When a President or CEO of a company assumes the position and title of leader, they then begin leading. He or she has in place resources and an infrastructure or team to provide guidance and direction on outcomes. Most of us will not be President, an Olympic Gold Medalist, or CEO of a Fortune 500 company. Most of us are leading before emerging as a leader.

Wright

The premise that you offered that everyone can be leading the way to success puts forth that someone will emerge as a leader when they identify a goal and move toward this objective. Would you say more about that emergence of someone as a leader?

Sabin

Leading for most of us is the primary access to being a leader. Leading is not hidden or passive. Even passive resistance is not passive. It takes raised awareness and conscious action. Those who are effective at *Leading the Way to Success* can name it, see it, own it, and claim it. Leading requires Commitment and Clarity with a capital C. We so desire to be part of something, to contribute, to grow, to develop and to accomplish, to have a commitment. Consider that the one common denominator integral to all leading is a clear identified outcome—a vision, purpose or objective. It crosses style, strengths, and skills. The desire, the intention to fulfill on an identified goal calls forth Leading. Substitute mission, vision, purpose, and dream, or goal for what I call an outcome. This precedes Leader for most of us. Like the saying that no one follows a parked car, if there is an absence of commitment to an objective, then there is a void and no leading. A

226

neighbor of mine determined to fit a new car in his garage cleaned it out in one weekend. The next weekend several other neighbors did the same!

In the mid-nineties, **10-year-old Aubyn Burnside** was horrified that children in the foster care system had to move all their possessions in garbage bags. She started asking for luggage donations for these children. Within six years Suitcases for Kids became an international nonprofit organization located in all 50 US states and 9 countries. First Leading then a Leader!

Wright

Suitcases for Kids is an excellent example. Here you share the story of a young girl who wished to help some children when she became aware of their sad situation. Aubyn's Burnsides intention was not to establish a worldwide nonprofit. It is a remarkable achievement. By first leading this young girl has become leader in the world and helped so many children all over the world.

Jennifer, earlier you referred to a myth being peeled away. What myth do you feel needs debunking?

Sabin

Many are under the illusion that leaders will not make mistakes—that they are flawless. That is a myth. Leaders do fail and will make mistakes. The Greeks had a phrase that translates very loosely: we can have no heroes if we are close enough to see the moles on their faces. Leaders make mistakes and poor choices. They are human beings. They are not infallible. They may have moles. The Leader is the one who recognizes it and takes responsibility for it and yet still keeps true to the vision, the purpose. A leader learns from failure.

There is no access to accomplishment without the risk of a mistake or failure.

Wright

Leaders may certainly make mistakes or demonstrate poor judgment. Since you earlier discussed the difference between leaders and leading, what does identifying and debunking this myth provide for those who are Leading?

Sabin

While Leading the way to success, we will certainly make mistakes and fail at times. Mistakes are a way to learn and grow, to get experience and to be wise. I do not know of anyone who has had success without failure or mistakes. A distinction of Leading is the ability to use failure as an opportunity to learn. Observe how people deal with failure—if they use it or let it use them. The wisest learn from others' failures ands mistakes by watching, listening, and reading. We will all reach this cross-road and will be faced with a choice. Do we hang up the "gone fishing" sign or do we let go of the experience and keep the lesson. Is it easy? No it is not. In his famous poem *If*, Rudyard Kipling wrote, "If you can meet with Triumph and Disaster and treat those two imposters just the same..." This is about being able to fail and make mistakes and not consider ourselves failures. Here is certainly a point in time where those leading begin the transformation process into leaders.

Wright

Jennifer, you shared earlier that after removing the myth of hubris there was a formula for leading the way to success. What is your formula?

Sabin

The formula is simple and like any formula it reduces the complex to the straightforward. It has three components. It starts at the end with Success. Since Success is the achievement of an identified objective, we need to determine the objective. Begin to speak it and get it out of our minds and into actual conversations. Simultaneously we need to create qualitative descriptions and quantitative measures. Here we establish the criteria so we know when the objective has been achieved. The quantitative can be measured: children, revenue, degrees, employees and so on. The qualitative is experienced: happiness, engaged, respected, pride and so on.

Do whatever it takes to have clarity and to own it: brainstorming, movies, books, coaches, executive thinking time, or mind maps, whatever is needed. Do we need to do *all* of the above? No. Of course we don't. It is our individual call. There is not a set time for this process to occur and it is really important we do not skip it. Even if we are supporting someone else's objective, it is still important to make it ours. The clarity, the focus, the commitment, the passion, the energy are what can be the difference between another good idea and a new reality. Can our objective, what we call success be articulated? If not, what is missing? Use this first part of the formula for desired outcome.

Wright

The first step of the formula is clear and understandable, and what are the hurdles and obstacles that can arise with this step?

Sabin

The biggest hurdle is when we gloss over this first part of the formula. This step distinguishes the societal "should" or "I am supposed to" from our individual desire and our "I want to." In this process we might identify limiting beliefs. We cannot change what we do not know about ourselves. This is valuable. Success involves generating something that has not existed previously for us. This really is the creation process of a new future.

Another pitfall is using references based in the past, which are comparative words. It is difficult say what "better" means and remove the actual words "better," "more," "bigger," "happier," "wealthier" from the description. When we quantify and qualify our objective without comparisons we are focused on the future.

Wright

Can you provide an example that demonstrates avoiding these pitfalls?

Sabin

Here's a quick example. A regional director of a sales team I had coached a few years prior contacted me for private client coaching. Successful and accomplished, she was completely stressed out. She shared that she wanted coaching to support her in eliminating stress and getting out of debt created by some poor money management habits. My company commitment is that each client is a success story and we mean it! So we chatted and within about ten minutes she created a new objective for our work together. Success to her was now to be proud of the way she handled her money and finances. She created a new future for herself that excited and inspired her and did not contain any comparisons. This is vastly different from fixing what is not working. This is basic example of what this step provides. Step one is simple and not always easy.

Wright

Let us suppose that the first step has been completed. What is the second step in this formula?

Sabin

Step one is future-based and step two is all about being in the present. In step two we identify the current reality objectively. This is the reality check. Dealing with the objective reality can be tough. We may need to take pictures, to use objective professionals, to review numbers and so on... This is solely about the facts. This step is where we press the pause button and acknowledge the facts that relate to our goal. Literally, if the accounts are frozen what is in the bank? If you put on the jeans in the closet would you wear them out of the house? If there is revenue from sales, what is the current overhead?

This is not for the faint of heart. It is very challenging to face the facts and to assess the current reality and not permit our emotions or our moods to influence or interfere. We are taking a snapshot and the camera only shows what it sees. The assessment is not about more, less, better, or worse. Lots of great work has been done in this step and this is not a function of time; it can take an hour or month.

David, to share an example of the potency of this part of the formula there was a division of a large organization that was floundering financially. In gathering the facts, absent of the story, the politics, and the emotions, the client learned that with each sale they were actually losing money. Interviews with the team made it clear that the objectives of the division were a complete mystery to most of the employees.

Do not skip this step! It is critical for illuminating the way to success.

Wright

So in step one the outcome is identified and in step two we learn the truth about today—the current state of affairs. What is step three?

Sabin

Step three is bridging the gap. Bridging the gap is the route, the way to reach our objective of Success. David, it is so simple and we make it so complex. That which is in currently in place, Step 2, is ideal to supports the current state as it is right now. When we want something other than what we have, change is required.

Step three is the Way. It is the plan, the route, the path. Step three is all about Leading. Leading the way is simpler given we know the destination, Step 1. Now we are guiding, directing, and living it ourselves. This step is about taking action—even imperfect action. Our route includes tactics, strategy, trust, learning, experiments, and mistakes. Time and time again I am blown away by the brilliance shown in bridging this gap. This is where we grow and experience pride and inspiration. Here we are involved with other people. We are engaged and participating in our life, not as an observer, not on the sidelines. It is in this arena where leading brings out the leader.

Wright

Is there anything else that needs to be addressed to support the formula?

Sabin

A formula is a reduction to a simple form. The three steps work. Here I would like to pull them together. Bottom line is for each of us to invest the critical thinking time for our definition of success. Own it, commit to it, and have it woven into the tapestry of our world view. Do the reality check. Put the current state of affairs on paper and identify the gap. Begin the active journey of bridging the gap—including planning, strategizing, taking actions, sharing, experimenting, failing, learning, and receiving. People will be drawn to us. Some will be supportive and some will not. We have clarity of our purpose and our objective. While diversions and distractions may slow us down, they will not stop us. We are certainly Leading the Way to Success and may be emerging as a leader.

My strong recommendation is to continually schedule reality checks to determine if we are on track. Do we still have our North Star—the identified objective which supports our purpose and leads us in the right direction?

Jennifer Sabin

Certainly for each of us there will be gaps and areas that we need support. Learn to celebrate while leading the way. Learn how to appreciate accomplishments along the way. Celebrating often by raising a glass, or with music, or a moment of quiet appreciation raises our awareness, confidence, esteem and pleasure. It creates momentum and balance. Also if we are leading, then we need to ensure that we taking care of our well being, basic self care, sleep and good food. There is a reason why pilots' daily hours in the air are limited. Would you want a sleep-deprived surgeon operating on you? Remember we are human. Also important is to remember the myth associated with leaders and not get deluded by the idea that we can enjoy or achieve success without failure or mistakes.

Leading the way to success is a ride of a lifetime. Start with step one and define success—select a goal, create a vision, or identify an objective and remember to pack up courage, compassion, and a sense of humor.

Wright

Jennifer, you have given perhaps a different view on leading the way to success. Is there anything else that you wanted to address in these final few minutes?

Sabin

Yes, even after my rather lengthy summation. This approach does make sense. To every man and woman who is considering the formula I ask of you what I request of our clients and program participants. Apply and experiment Try it, apply it, and live it. I hear over and over that knowledge is power and that is just not true. Knowledge is not power—*applied* knowledge is power.

Think about how many people know how to lose weight. Those who have the knowledge and could probably write a how-to book or host a talk show. Yet, how many of those who know, apply that knowledge? One setback, one failure, and we are stopped. If we break a dish we do not throw out the entire set of dishes. It really is the same—knowledge and skill have no power unless applied. All I have shared may make sense on paper yet it will not impact anyone's life unless implemented. The formula, as basic as it is, does work. For more than twenty years in more than twenty countries we at GMG, have been doing what works and this works.

David, as I shared in the beginning leading the way to success is inclusive not exclusive. It is available for everyone at anytime.

Wright

Well, what a great conversation. I really appreciate the time you've spent with me here today answering all these questions. You've created some space for me to think about some of these things you've been talking about. You're defining *Leading the Way Success* a little bit differently than I've heard it defined before.

Sabin

Well, thank you. This has been interesting and illuminating to me as well.

Wright

Today we've been talking with Jennifer Sabin, who is Founder and Managing Partner of the Growth Management Group, LLC. To date, the crowning achievement for Jennifer and her company was the realization of her vision with the international release of the " DTG Program Series, Daring to Grow™". It is an outstanding, affordable program series based on proven foundational theory. It was a dream of Jennifer's to create a platform to share her company's work, so that everyone who wants success, personal or professional, has access to achieve it and accomplish it without unnecessary stress and debt.

Jennifer, thank you so much for being with us today for *Leading the Way to Success.*

Sabin

Thank you, David; I have really enjoyed this conversation.

About the Author

Jennifer Sabin is the Founder and Managing Partner of the Growth Management Group LLC. For more than 20 years she has been an industry leader providing premium coaching and consulting services in more than 23 countries. She started out in the 80's as the youngest woman owning an American Stock Exchange seat and she rapidly expanded her firm into a premier international consulting and coaching company. She is deeply committed to the success of her clients from corporate to private individuals. In addition to working directly with may of the GMG clients she is a renowned speaker and lecturer and has addressed groups from Maine to Moscow.

Jennifer is also the lead program designer on the GMG LLC design team creating workshops, programs, seminars and private client work. She delivers programs that are always on the cutting edge of combining the philosophy of coaching and the pragmatism and expertise of business. Jennifer is the recipient of numerous awards including the New York Mayor's Volunteer Service Award for her consulting work with businesses impacted by the US tragedy on September 11, 2001. She served Girls Inc, National Advisory Board for Economic Literacy, she sat on the Congressional Organized Market 2000 Committee, and was invited to attend the 21st Century Summit in Washington DC, where she and other business leaders met with the President and discussed issues impacting women entrepreneurs. Jennifer holds the designation of PCC with the International Coach Federation and is an adjunct faculty member at Coach University. Jennifer has been recognized by the National Association of Women Business Owners (NAWBO) as a Tale of Triumph. Jennifer graduated from University of Pennsylvania, and continued her graduate work in Global Business Cultures at New York University in the John W. Draper Program. Jennifer currently lives in Palm Beach County Florida.

Jennifer Sabin
The Growth Management Group LLC
PO Box 2145
Palm Beach FL 33480
800-804-0461
jennifer@gmgglobal.com
www.gmgglobal.com